101

DISHES TO

eat

BEFORE
YOU
DIE(t)

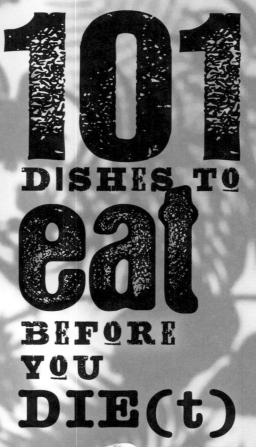

101 DISHES TO eat BEFORE YOU DIE(t)

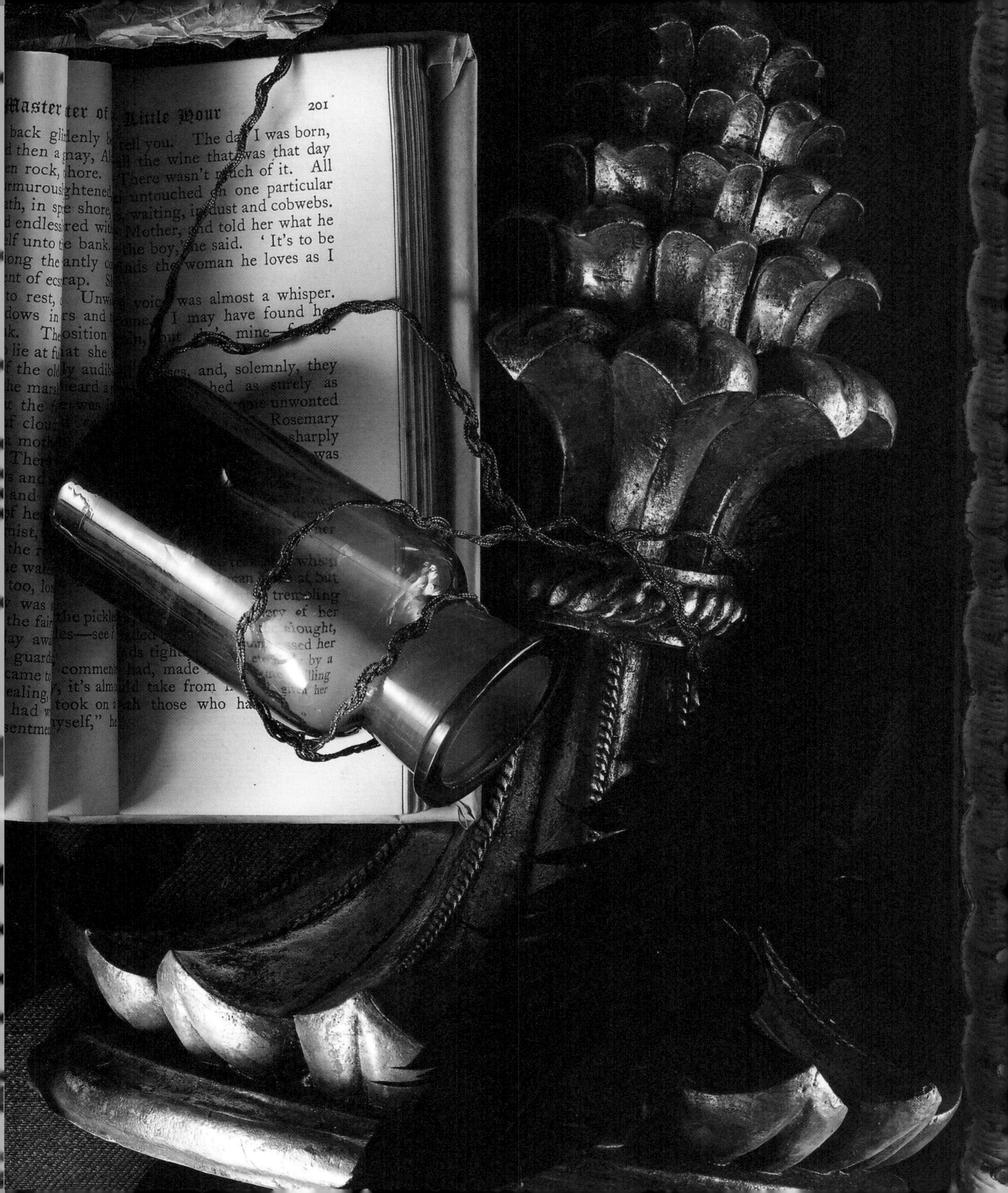

Contents

INTRODUCTION

101 ways to spoil yourself

Many of us have a distinct hankering for rich, carbohydrate-laden foods, rather than their lean, raw, virtuously spartan counterparts. Why is this, when it's so obvious which type is better for us?

One reason is that these foods are simply the most flavorsome. This is why processed foods marketed as "low-fat" often contain a raft of additives—because otherwise they would be distinctly lacking in flavor, and bland products are hard to sell, no matter how healthful they might be. Similarly, carbohydrates are filling, comforting, and sustaining for both body and soul—who couldn't like them?

Besides, we're conditioned to think of such foods as luxurious, comforting, decadent, and special. It's so tempting to have them every day—or even every meal. Feeling blue? Reach for the lasagna. Got something to celebrate? Make merry with beef Wellington. Feel like indulging yourself? Tuck into a big bowl of pasta.

With all these delectably naughty dishes around, it's no wonder so many of us regularly stray off the straight and narrow. After all, when it comes to starting that much-needed diet, there's always tomorrow.

NIBBLES, SNACKS, & things

IN SMALL PACKAGES

Serves 4

Beef nachos

oil, for cooking

14 ounces lean ground beef

1 onion, chopped

1–2 tablespoons chopped fresh chili

1 tablespoon ground cumin

3 teaspoons ground coriander

¼ cup concentrated tomato purée

½ cup bottled tomato pasta sauce or salsa

½ cup refried beans or 14 ounces tinned red kidney beans, drained and rinsed

corn chips, grated cheddar cheese and sour cream

chili powder, to sprinkle

Guacamole

1 ripe avocado

1 small onion, finely chopped

1 tomato, finely chopped

2 tablespoons chopped fresh cilantro

2–3 tablespoons sour cream

3–4 teaspoons lemon juice

Tabasco sauce, to taste

Heat a little oil in a frying pan and brown the beef in batches, stirring and breaking up any lumps with a fork or wooden spoon. Transfer to a bowl and set aside.

Add a little more oil to the pan, add the onion, chili, cumin, and coriander and stir over medium heat for 2–3 minutes. Return the beef to the pan and stir in the tomato purée, pasta sauce, and beans. Simmer for 5–10 minutes.

To make the guacamole, peel the avocado and coarsely mash the flesh in a bowl. Add the onion, tomato, cilantro, sour cream, and lemon juice. Mix well with a fork. Add some salt, freshly ground black pepper, and Tabasco to taste.

Spoon the beef into a large ovenproof dish. Arrange the corn chips around the mixture and sprinkle with the cheese. Place under a preheated broiler or in a moderate 350°F oven for 10-15 minutes, or until the cheese has melted. Top with the guacamole, a spoonful of sour cream, and a sprinkle of chili powder.

NOTE Traditionally, nachos were made with shredded cooked beef rather than ground meat.

Makes
20

Arancini

large pinch of saffron threads

I cup dry white wine

3 cups chicken stock

heaping ⅓ cup butter

I onion, finely chopped

I large garlic clove, crushed

2 tablespoons fresh thyme
    leaves

I cup risotto rice

½ cup freshly grated
    parmesan cheese

⅔ cup cubed fresh
    mozzarella or fontina
    cheese

scant ⅔ cup dry breadcrumbs

oil, for deep-frying

Soak the saffron in the wine while you prepare the risotto. Pour the stock into a saucepan and bring to the boil. Reduce the heat, cover with a lid, and keep at a low simmer.

Melt the butter in a large saucepan. Cook the onion and garlic over low heat for 3–4 minutes, or until softened but not browned. Add the thyme and rice to the onion and cook, stirring, for I minute. Add the wine and saffron and stir until the wine is all absorbed. Add ½ cup of the hot stock and stir constantly over medium heat until all the liquid is absorbed. Continue adding more stock, ½ cup at a time, until all the liquid is absorbed and the rice is tender and creamy; this will take 25–30 minutes. When making arancini, it is not essential to keep the rice al dente — if it is a little more glutinous, it will stick together better.

Remove the pan from the heat and stir in the parmesan, then spread the mixture out onto a tray covered with plastic wrap. Refrigerate to cool and firm up, preferably overnight.

To make the arancini, roll a small amount of risotto into a walnut-sized ball. Press a hole in the middle with your thumb, push a small piece of mozzarella or fontina cheese inside, and press the risotto around it to enclose it in a ball. Repeat with the rest of the risotto. Roll each ball in the breadcrumbs, pressing down to coat well.

Heat enough oil in a deep-fryer or large heavy-based saucepan to fully cover the arancini. Heat the oil to 350°F, or until a cube of bread dropped into the oil browns in 15 seconds. Cook the arancini in batches, without crowding, for 3–4 minutes. Drain on crumpled paper towels and leave for a couple of minutes before eating. Serve hot or at room temperature.

3

Makes
36

Stuffed black olives

36 pitted jumbo black or large kalamata olives (see Note)

heaping ⅓ cup goat's cheese

1 teaspoon capers, drained and finely chopped

1 clove garlic, crushed

2 tablespoons finely chopped fresh flat-leaf parsley

1½ tablespoons all-purpose flour

2 eggs, lightly beaten

1 cup dry breadcrumbs

oil, for deep-frying

lemon wedges, to serve

Carefully cut the olives along the open cavity so they are opened out, but still in one piece.

Mash the goat's cheese, capers, garlic, and half of the parsley together in a small bowl, then season with salt and black pepper. Push an even amount of the mixture into the cavity of the olives, then press them closed.

Put the flour in one small bowl, the egg in another, and combine the breadcrumbs and remaining parsley in a third. Dip each olive first into the flour, then into the egg, and finally into the breadcrumbs. Put the crumbed olives on a plate and refrigerate for at least 2 hours.

Fill a deep heavy-based saucepan or deep-fryer one-third full of oil and heat to 350°F, or until a cube of bread dropped into the oil browns in 15 seconds. Cook the olives in batches for 1–2 minutes, or until golden brown all over; you may need to turn them with tongs. Drain on crumpled paper towels and season. Serve warm or at room temperature with lemon wedges.

TIP The bigger the olives are, the easier they will be to handle. If you can't find large pitted olives, buy stuffed ones and remove the filling.

14

Quesadillas

1 tablespoon oil

1 pound ground chicken

1¼ ounce packet taco
   seasoning mix

½ cup tomato salsa

1 cup canned refried beans

2 cups grated low-fat tasty
   cheese

4 flour tortillas

sour cream, to serve

Heat the oil in a frying pan and cook the chicken, using
a fork to break up any lumps.

Add the taco seasoning and stir, cooking for 2 minutes.
Add the salsa. Stir until warmed through. Remove from
the heat.

In a small saucepan, heat the refried beans with
4 tablespoons of water until the mixture is thick.

To make the quesadillas, put some of the cheese on half of
each tortilla. Top with the chicken mixture, refried beans,
and more cheese.

Fold the top over and cook each one in a frying pan over
medium heat until browned on both sides. Serve hot with
a dollop of sour cream.

TIP Cheese is an essential
ingredients in quesadillas; their
name comes from "queso," the
Spanish word for cheese.

Fried cheese and ham sandwiches

⅓ cup unsalted butter

2 tablespoons all-purpose flour

¾ cup milk

½ teaspoon dijon mustard

1 egg yolk

grated nutmeg

12 slices white bread

6 slices ham

1¼ cups shredded gruyère cheese

Melt 2 tablespoons of the butter in a saucepan, add the flour, and stir over low heat for 3 minutes. Slowly add the milk and mustard, whisking constantly. Leave to simmer until the mixture has thickened and reduced by about a third. Remove from the heat and stir in the egg yolk. Season with salt, pepper, and nutmeg and leave to cool completely.

Place half the bread slices on a cookie sheet. Top each piece of bread with a slice of ham, then with some of the sauce, then gruyère, and finally with another piece of bread. Melt half the remaining butter in a large frying pan and fry the sandwiches on both sides until they are golden brown, adding the remaining butter when you need it. Cut each sandwich in half to serve.

Makes
18-20

Hushpuppies

¾ cup fine cornmeal

¼ cup all-purpose flour

1 tablespoon sugar

1 teaspoon baking powder

½ teaspoon baking soda

¼ teaspoon onion salt

¼ teaspoon chili powder

1 teaspoon Cajun spice mix

1 clove garlic, finely chopped

2 tablespoons grated onion

1 egg, lightly beaten

½ cup buttermilk

1 tablespoon water

oil, for deep-frying

In a mixing bowl, combine the cornmeal, flour, sugar, baking powder, baking soda, onion salt, chili powder, and Cajun spices. Add the garlic and grated onion.

Stir together the egg, buttermilk, and water, and pour over the dry mixture, and then stir until the dry ingredients are just moistened.

Heat oil in a deep, heavy-based pan until moderately hot (375°F) or until a cube of bread dropped in the oil takes 10 seconds to brown. Carefully spoon tablespoonfuls of batter into the hot oil. Cook until puffy and lightly golden, tuning each once or twice to cook evenly.

Remove from the oil with a slotted spoon or strainer. Drain on paper towels. Keep warm in a 325°F oven while frying the rest. Serve warm.

NOTE Cook only four or five hushpuppies at a time, as overcrowding in the pan will reduce the oil temperature and cause the hushpuppies to absorb excess oil. The depth of oil in the pan is important. There should be enough oil to cover the food completely by about 1 inch while it is cooking.

Empanadas

Serves 8

¼ cup olive oil

1⅔ cups finely diced onions

4 scallions, thinly sliced

3 garlic cloves, crushed

7 ounces ground beef

2 teaspoons ground cumin

2 teaspoons dried oregano

9 ounces potatoes, cut into small cubes

1 pound block ready-made puff pastry, thawed

½ cup chopped pitted black olives

2 hard-cooked eggs, finely chopped

1 egg, separated

pinch paprika

pinch sugar

Heat 1 tablespoon of the oil in a frying pan, add the onion and scallion, and stir over low heat for 5 minutes. Stir in the garlic and cook for 3 minutes. Remove from the pan.

Heat another tablespoon of oil in the pan, add the beef, and stir over medium heat until browned, breaking up any lumps with a fork. Return the onion mixture and stir well. Add the cumin, oregano, and 1 teaspoon each of salt and pepper, and stir for another 2 minutes. Transfer to a bowl and allow to cool. Wipe out the pan.

Heat the remaining oil in the pan, add the potato, and stir over high heat for 1 minute. Reduce the heat to low and stir for 5 minutes, or until tender. Transfer to a plate to cool. Gently mix the potato into the beef mixture. Preheat the oven to 400°F. Grease two cookie sheets.

Divide the pastry into two portions and roll out each piece on a lightly floured surface until ⅛ inch thick. Cut out rounds, using a 4-inch cutter.

Spoon the beef mixture onto one half of each pastry round, leaving a border all around. Place a few olive pieces and some chopped egg on top. Brush the pastry border with egg white. Fold each pastry over to make a half-moon shape, pressing firmly to seal. Press the edges with a floured fork, then transfer to the trays. Mix the egg yolk, paprika, and sugar, and brush over the empanadas. Bake for 15 minutes, or until golden.

Garlic shrimp

2 pounds 12 ounces
   uncooked shrimp

⅓ cup butter, melted

¾ cup olive oil

8 garlic cloves, crushed

2 scallions, thinly sliced

bread, to serve

As if these deep-fried shrimp themselves weren't irresistible enough, the garlic-flavored oil that they're cooked in is divine, just crying out for slice after slice of crusty bread to soak it up with.

Preheat the oven to 500°F. Peel the shrimp, leaving the tails intact. Gently pull out the vein from each shrimp back, starting at the head end. Cut a slit down the back of each shrimp.

Combine the butter and oil and divide among four 2-cup ovenproof pots. Divide half the crushed garlic evenly among the pots.

Place the pots on a cookie sheet and heat in the oven for 10 minutes, or until the mixture is bubbling. Divide the shrimp and remaining garlic among the pots. Return to the oven for 5 minutes, or until the shrimp are cooked. Stir in the scallion. Season to taste. Serve with bread to mop up the juices.

NOTE Garlic shrimp can also be made in a cast-iron frying pan in the oven or on the stovetop.

9

Makes
16

Cheese twists

1 sheet frozen puff pastry, thawed

1 egg, lightly beaten

¼ cup finely grated parmesan cheese

Preheat the oven to 415°F. Lay the thawed puff pastry on a work surface and brush lightly with beaten egg. Cut the pastry into ⅝ inch strips. Holding both ends, twist each strip in opposite directions twice.

Put the strips on a lightly greased cookie sheet. Sprinkle the parmesan over the flat part of the twists. Bake for 10 minutes, or until puffed and golden.

NOTE Cheese twists can be prepared several hours ahead. Refrigerate or freeze them on the trays, then put them in the oven just before you want to serve them.

Makes
40

Gyoza

1½ cups finely shredded Chinese cabbage

8 ounces ground pork

2 garlic cloves, finely chopped

2 teaspoons finely chopped fresh ginger

2 scallions, finely chopped

2 teaspoons cornstarch

1 tablespoon light soy sauce

2 teaspoons Chinese rice wine

2 teaspoons sesame oil

40 round Shanghai dumpling wrappers

2 tablespoons vegetable oil

½ cup chicken stock

soy sauce or Chinese black vinegar, to serve

Put the Chinese cabbage and ½ teaspoon salt in a colander, then sit the colander in a large bowl. Toss the cabbage, and then leave for 30 minutes to drain. Stir occasionally. This process will draw the liquid out of the cabbage and prevent the filling from becoming soggy.

Put the pork, garlic, ginger, scallion, cornflour, soy sauce, rice wine, and sesame oil in a bowl. Mix together with your hands.

Rinse the cabbage under cold running water. Press dry between layers of paper towel. Add to the pork mixture and combine well.

Place 1 teaspoon of the mixture in the center of each wrapper, brushing the inside edge of the wrapper with a little water. Bring the two edges of the wrapper together to form a semi-circle. Using your thumb and index finger, create a pleat, pressing firmly and gently tapping the gyoza on a work surface to form a flat bottom. Repeat with the remaining wrappers and filling.

Heat a quarter of the oil in a wok over medium–high heat. Working in four batches, cook the gyoza for 2 minutes, flat side down. Reduce the heat and add a quarter of the stock, shaking the wok gently to unstick the gyoza. Cover and steam for 4 minutes, or until the liquid has evaporated. Remove and keep warm. Repeat with the remaining oil, gyoza, and stock. Serve with soy sauce or Chinese black vinegar, for dipping.

Serves
8

Chicken liver and grand marnier pâté

1 pound 10 ounces chicken livers, well trimmed

1 cup milk

heaping ¾ cup butter, softened

4 scallions, finely chopped

1 tablespoon Grand Marnier

1 tablespoon frozen orange juice concentrate, thawed

salt and freshly ground pepper

½ orange, very thinly sliced

toast or crackers, to serve

Jellied layer

1 tablespoon orange juice concentrate

1 tablespoon Grand Marnier

1¼ cups canned chicken consommé, undiluted

2½ teaspoons powdered gelatine

Combine the chicken livers and milk in a bowl. Cover and refrigerate for 1 hour. Drain the livers and discard the milk. Rinse in cold water, drain, and pat dry with paper towels.

Melt a third of the butter in a frying pan, add the scallion, and cook over low heat for 2–3 minutes, or until tender, but not brown. Add the livers and cook, stirring, over medium heat for 4–5 minutes, or until just cooked. Remove from the heat and cool a little.

In a food processor, process the livers until very smooth. Add the remaining butter to the processor with the Grand Marnier and orange juice concentrate and process until creamy. Season to taste with salt and black pepper. Transfer to a 5-cup serving dish, cover the surface with plastic wrap, and chill for 1½ hours, or until firm.

For the jellied layer, whisk together the orange juice concentrate, Grand Marnier, and ½ cup of the consommé in a jug. Sprinkle the gelatin over the liquid in an even layer and leave until the gelatin is spongy — do not stir. Heat the remaining consommé in a pan, remove from the heat, and add the gelatin mixture. Stir to dissolve the gelatin, then leave to cool and thicken to the consistency of uncooked egg white, but not set.

Press the orange slices lightly into the surface of the pâté and spoon the thickened jelly evenly over the top. Refrigerate until set. Serve at room temperature with toast or crackers.

12

Makes
16

Ham and pineapple pizza wheels

oil, for brushing

2 cups self-rising flour

3 tablespoons butter, chopped

½ cup milk

⅓ cup concentrated tomato purée

2 small onions, finely chopped

4 pineapple slices, finely chopped

1⅓ cups shredded ham

¾ cup shredded cheddar cheese

2 tablespoons finely chopped flat-leaf parsley

Preheat the oven to 350°F. Brush two cookie sheets with oil. Sift the flour into a bowl. Using your fingertips, rub in the butter until the mixture resembles fine breadcrumbs. Make a well in the center and add almost all the milk. Mix with a flat-bladed knife, using a cutting action, until the mixture comes together in beads. Gather into a ball and turn out onto a lightly floured work surface.

Divide the dough in half. Roll out each half on baking paper to an 8 x 12-inch rectangle, about ¼ inch thick. Spread half of the tomato purée over each rectangle, leaving a ½-inch border.

Mix the onion, pineapple, ham, cheddar, and parsley. Spread evenly over the tomato paste, leaving a ¾-inch border. Using the paper as a guide, roll up the dough from the long side.

Cut each roll into eight even slices. Place the slices on the trays and bake for 20 minutes, or until golden. Serve warm.

Makes
30

Honey-garlic ribs

3 pounds 5 ounces
American-style pork
spare ribs

½ cup honey

6 garlic cloves, crushed

2 inch piece fresh ginger,
finely grated

¼ teaspoon Tabasco sauce

¼ cup chili sauce

2 teaspoons grated orange zest

Cut the ribs into small pieces, with one or two bones per piece. Put the ribs in a large dish. Combine the remaining ingredients and pour over the ribs. Stir until well coated. Refrigerate for several hours, or overnight.

Preheat the oven to 400°F. Drain the ribs and place the marinade in a small saucepan. Put the ribs in one or two large shallow roasting pans in a single layer. Bring the marinade to the boil and simmer gently for 3–4 minutes, or until it has thickened and reduced slightly.

Brush the ribs with the marinade and bake for 50 minutes, basting with the marinade three or four times. Cook until the ribs are well browned and tender. Serve hot with any remaining marinade.

NOTE Any mixture that has been used to marinate meat, fish, or poultry needs to be brought to a boil and cooked for several minutes if you then want to use it as a sauce on the cooked meat. This process will kill any potential pathogens in the mixture.

Serves
4

Corn pancakes
with bacon and maple syrup

¾ cup self-rising flour

¾ cup fine cornmeal

1 cup milk

1½ cups sweet corn kernels
(about 3 cobs)

olive oil, for frying

8 bacon slices

½ cup maple syrup

While one plain pancake on its own is not really a diet buster, the type that is studded with creamy corn and served with plenty of bacon and maple syrup is in another realm altogether.

Sift the flour into a bowl and stir in the cornmeal. Add the milk and corn and stir until just combined, adding more milk if the batter is too dry. Season with salt and pepper.

Heat the oil in a large frying pan and spoon half the batter into the pan in batches, making four 3½-inch pancakes. Cook for 2 minutes on each side, or until golden. Repeat with the remaining batter. Keep warm on a plate in a 235°F oven while cooking the bacon. Add the bacon to the pan and cook for 5 minutes. Put two pancakes and two bacon slices on each plate and drizzle with maple syrup, to serve.

Serves
8

Bagels

2 teaspoons dried yeast

1 teaspoon sugar

1 tablespoon barley malt
syrup or honey

4 cups white bread flour

2 teaspoons salt

coarse cornmeal, to dust

Put the yeast, sugar, barley malt syrup, and 1½ cups warm water in a small bowl and stir until dissolved. Leave in a warm place for 10 minutes, or until the mixture is frothy and slightly increased in volume.

Put half of the flour in a large bowl, make a well in the center, and add the yeast mixture and salt. Stir with a wooden spoon, adding more flour if needed to make a firm dough. Turn out onto a floured work surface and knead for 10–12 minutes, or until smooth and stiff. Add more flour if needed, to make the dough quite stiff, then divide into eight portions and roll into smooth balls. Cover with plastic wrap or a clean cloth and leave for 5 minutes.

Roll each ball under your palms to form a rope 12 inches long, without tapering the ends. Dampen the ends slightly, overlap by 1½ inches and pinch firmly together. Place one at a time around the base of your fingers and, with the overlap under your palm, roll the rope several times. Apply firm pressure to seal the seam. It should be the same thickness all the way around. Place all the balls on polenta-dusted cookie sheets, cover with plastic wrap, and refrigerate for 12 hours.

Preheat the oven to 475°F. Line two cookie sheets with baking paper. Remove the bagels from the refrigerator 20 minutes before baking. Bring a large saucepan of water to the boil and drop the bagels, in batches of three or four, into the water for 30 seconds. Remove and drain, base-down, on a wire rack. Place the bagels on the cookie sheets and bake for 15 minutes, or until deep golden brown and crisp. Cool on a wire rack.

16

Serves
4

Asparagus
with citrus hollandaise

24 asparagus spears, woody
ends trimmed

¾ cup butter

4 egg yolks

1–2 tablespoons lemon,
lime, or orange juice

shavings of parmesan or
pecorino cheese (optional)

There's nothing unhealthy about asparagus; not the slightest thing. That's why we recommend dressing it up with an eggy, buttery sauce with a citrus tang.

Put the asparagus in a saucepan of boiling water. Simmer for 2–4 minutes, or until just tender. Drain well.

Melt the butter in a small saucepan. Skim any froth from the top and discard. Allow the butter to cool.

Combine the egg yolks and 2 tablespoons water in a small saucepan and whisk for 30 seconds, or until pale and creamy. Place the pan over very low heat and continue whisking for 3 minutes, or until the mixture thickens.

Remove from the heat. Add the cooled butter gradually, whisking constantly (leave the whey in the bottom of the pan). Stir in the lemon, lime, or orange juice and season to taste. Drizzle the sauce over the asparagus, sprinkle with black pepper, and garnish with cheese shavings (if desired).

Serves
6

Oysters mornay

24 oysters in their shells

3 tablespoons butter

1 shallot, finely chopped

2 tablespoons all-purpose flour

1½ cups milk

pinch of nutmeg

½ bay leaf

¼ cup gruyère cheese, grated

¼ cup parmesan cheese, grated, plus a little extra for broiling

Shuck the oysters, reserving all the liquid. Strain the liquid into a saucepan. Rinse the oysters to remove any bits of shell. Wash and dry the shells.

Melt half of the butter in another saucepan, add the shallot, and cook, stirring, for 3 minutes. Stir in the flour to make a roux and stir over very low heat for 3 minutes without allowing the roux to brown. Remove from the heat and add the milk gradually, stirring after each addition until smooth. Return to the heat, add the nutmeg and bay leaf, and simmer for 5 minutes. Strain through a fine sieve into a clean pan.

Heat the oyster liquid in the saucepan to a simmer (add a little water if you need more liquid). Add the oysters and poach for 30 seconds, then lift them out with a slotted spoon and place them back into their shells. Stir the cooking liquid into the sauce. Add the cheeses and remaining butter, and stir until they have melted into the sauce. Season with salt and pepper. Preheat the broiler.

Spoon a little sauce over each oyster, sprinkle with parmesan, and place under the hot broiler for a couple of minutes, or until golden.

Makes
12

Pan-fried cheese slices

8 ounces kefalograviera
(see Note) or haloumi

2 tablespoons all-purpose
flour

¼ cup olive oil

½ teaspoon dried oregano

½ lemon, cut into wedges,
for serving

bread, for serving

Frying makes so many foods even more delicious, and some types of cheese are no exception. These little morsels are so tasty it's tempting to eat them straight out of the pan.

Cut the cheese into ½ inch slices and then into pieces. The pieces can be as large as you wish, as they can be cut smaller for serving.

Put the flour in a shallow dish and season well with cracked pepper. Toss the cheese in the flour. Heat the oil over high heat in a frying pan until hot. Add the cheese to the pan and cook for 1 minute, or until browned and crusty underneath. Carefully turn the cheese to brown the other side. Lift onto a serving plate and sprinkle with oregano. Serve hot with lemon wedges and fresh bread.

NOTE Kefalograviera and the similar kefalotyri are pale, hard sheep's milk cheeses originating in Greece.

19

Fried potatoes
with garlic mayonnaise

1 pound 10 ounces all-
  purpose potatoes, peeled
¼ cup olive oil

Garlic mayonnaise
2 egg yolks
4 garlic cloves, crushed
¼ cup white wine vinegar or
  lemon juice
1 cup mild olive oil

The source of the calories here is obvious—potatoes and oil, basically, spiced up with a good hit of garlic. Simple and very, very moreish.

Preheat the oven to 400°F. Cut the potatoes into 1½-inch cubes and put on a cookie sheet with the olive oil. Mix to coat and season well. Cook in the oven for 45 minutes, or until golden. Shake the cookie sheet occasionally so the potatoes bake evenly on all sides.

To make the mayonnaise, put the egg yolks, garlic, and half of the vinegar or lemon juice in a bowl. Using a balloon whisk, or electric beaters, whisk until well combined. While you continuously whisk, gradually add the oil in a slow stream until you have a thick mayonnaise. If at some point the mayonnaise becomes too thick, add the remaining vinegar and continue adding the rest of the oil. Season well.

Season the potatoes and serve with the garlic mayonnaise dolloped over the top or served on the side for dipping. Any leftover garlic mayonnaise will keep in an airtight container in the refrigerator for 2–3 days.

20

Mini corn dogs

Makes
16

8 large frankfurters

8 wooden skewers

cornstarch, for dusting

oil, for deep-frying

tomato ketchup, for dipping

Batter

1¾ cups self-rising flour

¼ cup cornmeal

1 egg, lightly beaten

1 tablespoon oil

12 fl oz water

Cut the frankfurters in half crossways. Cut the skewers in half and insert one half through each frankfurter, leaving some of the skewer sticking out for a handle. Dust the frankfurters with a little cornstarch.

To make the batter, sift the flour into a large bowl, stir in the cornmeal, and make a well in the center. Gradually add the combined egg, oil, and 12 fl oz water, whisking to make a smooth, lump-free batter.

Fill a deep, heavy-based pan one-third full of oil and heat to 350°F. The oil is ready when a cube of bread dropped into the oil turns golden brown in 15 seconds. Dip the frankfurters into the batter a few at a time; drain off the excess batter. Using tongs, gently lower the frankfurters into the oil. Cook over medium–high heat for 1–2 minutes, or until golden and crisp and heated through. Carefully remove from the oil. Drain on crumpled paper towel and keep warm. Repeat with the remaining frankfurters. Serve with tomato ketchup.

NOTE You can add a teaspoon of chopped fresh chili or a pinch of chili powder to the batter if you want a spicier corn dog.

Makes
20

Peking duck with mandarin pancakes

One duck, about 3 pounds 8 ounces

1 tablespoon honey

12 scallions

2 tablespoons hoisin sauce

1 small short cucumber, seeds removed, flesh diced into matchsticks

Mandarin pancakes

2½ cups all-purpose flour

2 teaspoons superfine sugar

1 tablespoon sesame oil

Wash the duck, and remove the neck and any large pieces of fat from inside the carcass. Hold the duck over the sink (wear thick rubber gloves to protect your hands) and very carefully and slowly pour 12 cups of boiling water over it, rotating the duck so the water scalds all the skin. You may need another lot of boiling water.

Put the duck on a cake rack placed over a baking pan. Mix the honey and ½ cup hot water and brush two coats of this glaze over the duck, to cover it completely. Dry the duck, preferably hanging it up in a cool, airy place. (Or use an electric fan on a cool setting, positioned about 1 yard away.) The skin is sufficiently dry when it is papery to touch. This may take 2–4 hours.

Take a 3-inch section from each scallion and make fine parallel cuts from the center towards the end. Place in iced water—the scallions will open into "brushes."

Preheat the oven to 415°F. Bake the duck on the rack over a baking pan for 30 minutes. Turn the duck over carefully, without tearing the skin, then bake for another 30 minutes. Remove and then leave for a minute or two. Place on a warm dish.

To make the pancakes, combine the flour and sugar in a bowl and pour in 1 cup boiling water. Stir a few times to just combine and leave until lukewarm. Knead the mixture on a lightly floured surface to make a smooth dough, cover, and set aside for 30 minutes.

Roll two level tablespoons of dough at a time into balls, then brush out to 3-inch rounds. Lightly brush one round with sesame oil and place another on top. Re-roll to make a thin pancake about 6 inches in diameter. Repeat with the remaining dough and oil to make about 10 "double" pancakes.

Heat a frying pan and cook the pancakes one at a time. When small bubbles appear on the surface, turn over and cook the second side, pressing the surface with a clean tea towel. The pancakes should puff up when done. Transfer to a plate. When cool enough to handle, peel each pair in two, stack on a plate, and cover at once to prevent them from drying out.

To serve, remove the crisp skin from the underside of the duck and cut into thin strips. Thinly slice the breast and leg meat and place on a warm serving plate. Arrange the cucumber sticks and scallion brushes on a serving plate. Pour the hoisin sauce into a small dish. Place the pancakes and finely sliced duck on separate plates. Each person takes a pancake, spreads a little sauce on it using the scallion brush, and adds a couple of pieces of cucumber, a scallion brush, and finally a piece of duck and crisp duck skin. The pancake is then folded over into an envelope shape to enclose the filling. Repeat the procedure for the remaining pancakes and duck.

NOTE Barbecued ducks are available at Asian barbecue stores, and ready-made pancakes are also available when you buy the duck.

Serves
10–12

Caramelized onion and potato salad

2 tablespoons oil

6 red onions, thinly sliced

2 pounds 4 ounces Kipfler, Desiree, or Pontiac potatoes

4 bacon slices

¾ cup chopped chives

Dressing

1 cup whole-egg mayonnaise

1 tablespoon Dijon mustard

2–3 tablespoons lemon juice

2 tablespoons sour cream

The word "salad" conjures visions of worthy greens and masses of raw vegetables, but it needn't be like that. Base a salad on potatoes, bacon, and a particularly rich dressing, and you could use it to derail any diet.

Heat the oil in a large heavy-based frying pan, add the onion, and cook over low–medium heat for 40 minutes, or until caramelized.

Cut the potatoes into large chunks (if small, leave them whole) and steam or boil for 5–10 minutes until just tender (pierce them with the point of a small knife — if the potato comes away easily, it is ready). Drain and cool slightly.

Remove the rind from the bacon and broil until crisp. Drain on crumpled paper towels and cool slightly before roughly chopping.

Put the potato, onion, and chives in a large bowl, reserving a few chives for garnish, and toss to combine.

To make the mayonnaise, whisk the ingredients together in a bowl. Pour over the salad and toss to coat. Sprinkle with the bacon and garnish with the reserved chives.

23

Hash browns

1 pound 12 ounces waxy potatoes (such as Desiree or Pontiac), peeled

½ cup butter

Boil or steam the potatoes until just tender. Drain, cool, chop coarsely or shred, and season with salt and freshly ground black pepper.

Heat half the butter in a large, heavy-based frying pan and put four lightly greased egg rings into the pan. Spoon the potato evenly into the egg rings, filling the rings to the top and pressing the potato down lightly to form flat cakes. Cook over medium-low heat for 5–7 minutes, or until a crust forms on the bottom. Be careful not to burn. Shake the pan gently to prevent sticking.

Turn the hash browns with a large spatula. Gently loosen the egg rings and remove with tongs. Cook for another 4–5 minutes, or until browned and crisp. Remove from the pan and drain on paper towels. Add a little more butter to the pan, if necessary, and cook the remaining potato in the same way. Serve immediately.

NOTE If you don't have egg rings, cook the potato mixture as one large cake in a frying pan. To turn it, loosen the mixture with a spatula, then place a large plate over the pan and carefully turn both pan and plate over so that the potato cake is inverted. Slide the cake off the plate and back into the pan and continue cooking until the underside is browned.

24

Makes
36

Shrimp toasts

To make the dipping sauce, combine the tomato ketchup, garlic, chilies, hoisin sauce, and Worcestershire sauce in a small bowl. Set aside until ready to serve.

Peel the shrimp and gently pull out the dark vein from each shrimp back, starting from the head end. Put the shrimp in a food processor with the garlic, water chestnuts, cilantro, ginger, egg whites, white pepper, and ¼ teaspoon salt and process for 20–30 seconds, or until smooth.

Brush the top of each slice of bread with lightly beaten egg yolk, then spread evenly with the shrimp mixture. Sprinkle generously with sesame seeds, pressing them down gently. Cut each slice of bread into three even strips.

Fill a wok or deep heavy-based saucepan one-third full of oil and heat to 350°F, or until a cube of bread dropped into the oil browns in 15 seconds. Starting with the shrimp mixture face down, deep-fry the toasts in small batches for 10–15 seconds, or until golden and crisp, turning the toasts over halfway through. Remove with tongs or a slotted spoon and drain on crumpled paper. Serve with the dipping sauce.

Dipping sauce

½ cup tomato ketchup

2 garlic cloves, crushed

2 small red chilies, seeded and finely chopped

2 tablespoons hoisin sauce

2 teaspoons Worcestershire sauce

12 ounces uncooked shrimp

1 garlic clove, chopped

heaping ⅓ cup canned water chestnuts, drained

1 tablespoon chopped cilantro leaves

¾ inch piece ginger, roughly chopped

2 eggs, separated

¼ teaspoon white pepper

12 slices white bread, crusts removed

1 cup sesame seeds

oil, for deep-frying

Pork and fennel sausage baguette with onion relish

Sausages

1 pound 10 ounces ground pork

½ cup fresh breadcrumbs

2 garlic cloves, crushed

3 teaspoons fennel seeds, coarsely crushed

1 teaspoon finely grated orange zest

2 teaspoons chopped thyme

2 large handfuls flat-leaf parsley, chopped

Onion relish

3 tablespoons butter

2 red onions, thinly sliced

1 tablespoon soft brown sugar

2 tablespoons balsamic vinegar

oil, for brushing

1 long baguette, cut into 4 pieces, or 4 long, crusty rolls

3 tablespoons, softened

2 handfuls arugula leaves

1 tablespoon extra virgin olive oil

1 teaspoon balsamic vinegar

Put the pork, breadcrumbs, garlic, fennel seeds, orange zest, thyme, and parsley in a large bowl, season well with salt and freshly ground black pepper, and mix together with your hands. Cover the mixture and refrigerate for 4 hours or overnight to allow the flavors to develop.

To make the onion relish, melt the butter in a heavy-based saucepan over low heat, add the onion, and cook, stirring occasionally, over low heat for 10 minutes, or until the onion is softened, but not browned. Add the brown sugar and vinegar, and continue to cook for another 30 minutes, stirring regularly.

Preheat a barbecue hotplate to medium direct heat. Divide the pork mixture into eight portions and use wet hands to mold each portion into a flattish sausage shape. Lightly brush the sausages with oil and cook for 8 minutes on each side, or until they are cooked through.

To assemble, split the baguette or rolls down the middle and butter them. Toss the arugula with the olive oil and balsamic vinegar, and put some of the leaves in each of the rolls. Top with a sausage and some of the onion relish.

Serves
4

Golden potato wedges

1 pound all-purpose potatoes

3 cups oil

sea salt and malt vinegar, to serve (optional)

The simplest things in life are often the best, so the saying goes. They can also be the naughtiest, at least in the case of this diet-destroying favorite. Just potatoes and oil. Divine.

Cut the potatoes into thick country-style chips or wedges. Heat the oil in a saucepan and cook the potatoes in batches until lightly golden. Drain on paper towels. Repeat with the remaining potatoes.

Just before serving, re-fry the potatoes in batches until crisp and golden. Sprinkle with sea salt and malt vinegar, if desired.

NOTE Frying chips or wedges twice ensures a fluffy interior and crisp exterior. Always deep-fry chips (and other foods) in batches so as not to reduce the temperature of the oil too much, and so that the foods being fried have plenty of room to move about and be turned.

Serves 6

Salt and pepper squid

2 pounds squid tubes, halved lengthways

1 cup lemon juice

2 cups cornstarch

1 tablespoon ground white pepper

2 teaspoons superfine sugar

4 egg whites, lightly beaten

oil, for deep-frying

lemon wedges, to serve

cilantro leaves, to garnish

Open out the squid tubes, wash them, and pat dry. Lay them on a chopping board with the inside facing upwards. Score a fine diamond pattern on the squid, being careful not to cut all the way through. Cut into 2 x 1¼ inch pieces. Place in a flat non-metallic dish, pour the lemon juice over, cover, and refrigerate for 15 minutes. Drain and pat dry.

Combine the cornstarch, 1 tablespoon salt, white pepper, and sugar in a bowl. Dip the squid into the egg white and dust with the flour mixture.

Fill a wok or deep, heavy-based saucepan one-third full of oil and heat to 350°F, or until a cube of bread dropped into the oil browns in 15 seconds. Deep-fry the squid in batches for 1–2 minutes, or until the squid turns white and curls. Drain on crumpled paper towel and serve immediately with lemon wedges, and garnished with coriander leaves.

Makes
24

Potato and coriander samosas

3 tablespoons butter

2 teaspoons grated fresh ginger

2 teaspoons cumin seeds

1 teaspoon hot curry powder

½ teaspoon garam masala

1 pound boiling potatoes, peeled and finely diced

¼ cup golden raisins

⅔ cup frozen baby peas

1 very large handful cilantro leaves

3 scallions, sliced

1 egg, lightly beaten

oil, for deep-frying

thick plain yogurt, to serve

Samosa pastry

3 cups all-purpose flour, sifted

1 teaspoon baking powder

scant ½ cup butter, melted

½ cup thick plain yogurt

Heat the butter in a large nonstick frying pan, add the ginger, cumin seeds, curry powder, and garam masala, and fry lightly for 1 minute. Add the potato and 3 tablespoons water and cook over low heat for 15–20 minutes, or until the potato is tender. Toss the golden raisins, peas, coriander and scallion through the potato, remove from the heat, and set aside to cool.

To make the samosa pastry, combine the flour, baking powder, and 1½ teaspoons salt in a large bowl. Make a well in the center and add the butter, yogurt, and ¾ cup water. Using a flat-bladed knife, bring the dough together. Turn out onto a lightly floured surface and bring together to form a smooth ball. Divide the dough into four. Roll one piece out until it is very thin. Cover the remaining pastry until you are ready to use it.

Using a 4½-inch diameter bowl as a guide, cut out six circles. Place a tablespoon of potato filling in the center of each circle, brush the edges of the pastry with egg, and fold over to form a semi-circle. Make repeated folds on the rounded edge by folding a little piece of the pastry back as you move around the edge. Continue with the remaining pastry and filling.

Heat the oil in a deep heavy-based pan to 350°F. It is important not to have the oil too hot or the samosas will burn before the pastry has cooked. Add the samosas two or three at a time and cook until golden. Drain on paper towels. Serve with yogurt.

29

Makes
36

Sausage rolls

These schoolyard favorites are popular with all ages, and homemade ones are so much tastier than the bought variety. And if you freeze them, they're always on hand to be popped in the oven for an impromptu feast.

3 sheets frozen puff pastry, thawed

2 eggs, lightly beaten

1 pound 10 ounces ground sausage

1 onion, finely chopped

1 garlic clove, crushed

1 cup fresh breadcrumbs

3 tablespoons chopped flat-leaf parsley

3 tablespoons chopped thyme

½ teaspoon ground sage

½ teaspoon freshly grated nutmeg

½ teaspoon ground cloves

Preheat the oven to 400°F. Lightly grease two cookie sheets.

Cut the pastry sheets in half and lightly brush the edges with some of the beaten egg.

Mix half the remaining egg with the remaining ingredients and ½ teaspoon black pepper in a large bowl, then divide into six even portions. Pipe or spoon the filling down the center of each piece of pastry, then brush the edges with some of the egg. Fold the pastry over the filling, overlapping the edges and placing the join underneath. Brush the rolls with more egg, then cut each into six short pieces.

Cut two small slashes on top of each roll, place on the cookie sheets, and bake for 15 minutes. Reduce the heat to 350°F and bake for another 15 minutes, or until puffed and golden.

TIP Sausage rolls can be made ahead for convenience; freeze them on cookie sheets then transfer to zip-lock plastic bags. Bake them unthawed and serve piping hot.

Cajun popcorn shrimp

1 pound 8 ounces large
   uncooked shrimp

1 egg

1¼ cups milk

⅓ cup fine cornmeal

1 cup all-purpose flour

½ teaspoon baking powder

4 teaspoons Cajun spice mix

¼ teaspoon dried basil

½ teaspoon celery salt

oil, for deep frying

Why are they called popcorn shrimp? Possibly because, just like popcorn, they're all too easy to demolish by the bucketload.

Peel and devein the shrimp. Rinse and dry well with paper towels.

Beat the egg and milk together. In a large bowl, combine the cornmeal, flour, baking powder, Cajun spices, basil, and celery salt. Add half the beaten egg mixture and mix to a smooth paste. Add the remaining egg mixture, mix well, and leave to stand for 30 minutes.

Dip the shrimp into the batter and deep-fry in small batches in moderately hot oil 375°F, until crisp and lightly golden. Remove with a slotted spoon or strainer.

Drain briefly on paper towel and serve hot with a sauce of your choice.

NOTE Use fine cornmeal in the batter mixture to make the shrimp extra crisp.

Buffalo chicken wings with ranch dressing

8 large chicken wings

2 teaspoons garlic salt

2 teaspoons onion powder

olive oil, for deep-frying

½ cup tomato ketchup

2 tablespoons Worcestershire sauce

1 tablespoon melted butter

2 teaspoons sugar

Tabasco sauce, to taste

Ranch dressing

½ cup mayonnaise

½ cup sour cream

2 tablespoons lemon juice

2 tablespoons snipped chives

Wash the wings thoroughly and pat dry with paper towels. Cut the tip off each wing and discard. Bend each wing back to snap the joint and cut through to create two pieces. Combine 2 teaspoons of black pepper, the garlic salt, and onion powder, and rub into the wings.

Heat the oil to moderately hot in a deep heavy-based pan. Deep-fry the chicken in batches for 2 minutes. Drain on paper towels.

Transfer the chicken to a shallow, nonmetallic dish. Combine the sauces, butter, sugar, and Tabasco and pour over the chicken, stirring to coat. Cover and refrigerate for at least 3 hours.

Cook the chicken on a hot, lightly oiled barbecue grill plate or flat plate for 5 minutes, turning and brushing with the marinade.

To make the ranch dressing, combine the mayonnaise, cream, juice, chives, and salt and pepper to taste, and serve with the chicken wings.

32

Serves
4

New Orleans oysters

24 large oysters, shells removed

2 teaspoons Cajun spice mix

½ teaspoon sweet paprika

½ teaspoon dried basil

½ cup all-purpose flour

½ cup vegetable oil

3 tablespoons unsalted butter

lemon wedges and mayonnaise, to serve

Rinse and dry the oysters. In a shallow dish, mix the Cajun spices, paprika, and basil thoroughly. Set aside two teaspoons of the spice mix. Add the flour to the remainder and stir thoroughly.

Thread three oysters onto eight oiled skewers (choose thin bamboo or metal) and coat with the spiced flour.

Heat the oil and butter in a large frying pan. Cook the oysters until they are golden, turning frequently. Drain on paper towels. Sprinkle with the reserve Cajun spices and serve with wedges of lemon and a dish of mayonnaise.

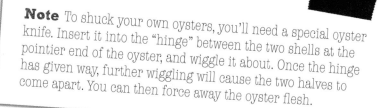

Note To shuck your own oysters, you'll need a special oyster knife. Insert it into the "hinge" between the two shells at the pointier end of the oyster, and wiggle it about. Once the hinge has given way, further wiggling will cause the two halves to come apart. You can then force away the oyster flesh.

Chinese spring rolls

2 dried shiitake mushrooms

9 ounces ground pork

1½ tablespoons dark soy sauce

2 teaspoons dry sherry

½ teaspoon Chinese
five-spice powder

2 tablespoons cornstarch,
plus 1½ teaspoons extra

⅓ cup peanut oil

½ celery stalk, finely chopped

2 scallions, thinly sliced

2 tablespoons canned
bamboo shoots, finely
sliced

¾ cup shredded Chinese
cabbage (wong bok)

2 garlic cloves, crushed

2 teaspoons finely chopped
fresh ginger

¼ teaspoon sugar

¼ teaspoon sesame oil

One 9 ounce packet 4½-inch
square spring roll wrappers

oil, for deep-frying

It's not the actual filling that's so bad here but the fact that they're deep-fried, and that it's so hard to stop at one. Or even several.

Put the shiitake mushrooms in a heatproof bowl, cover with boiling water, and soak for 20 minutes. Squeeze the mushrooms dry, discard the stems, and thinly slice the caps.

Mix the pork, soy sauce, sherry, five-spice, and 1 tablespoon of the cornstarch in a nonmetallic bowl. Allow to stand for 15 minutes.

Heat 2 tablespoons of the peanut oil in a wok over high heat until nearly smoking, then add the celery, scallion, bamboo shoots, and cabbage and stir-fry for 3–4 minutes, or until just soft. Season with salt, then transfer to a bowl and set aside.

Heat the remaining peanut oil in the wok and cook the garlic and ginger for 30 seconds. Add the pork mixture and stir-fry for 2–3 minutes, or until nearly cooked. Combine 1½ teaspoons of the cornstarch with ¼ cup water. Return the cooked vegetables to the wok, then stir in the mushrooms. Add the sugar, sesame oil, and cornstarch mixture, and stir for 2 minutes. Remove from the heat and cool.

To make the dipping sauce, combine the soy sauce, hoisin sauce, plum sauce, sweet chili sauce, and ⅓ cup water in a bowl, and stir to combine.

Make a paste by stirring 2–3 teaspoons cold water into the remaining cornstarch. Place a spring roll wrapper on a work surface, with one corner pointing towards you. Put 2 teaspoons of the filling in the center of the wrapper, then brush the edges with a little cornstarch paste. Roll up, tucking in the sides as you do so. Repeat with the remaining filling and wrappers.

Fill a wok or deep, heavy-based saucepan one-third full of oil and heat to 350°F, or until a cube of bread dropped into the oil browns in 15 seconds. Deep-fry the spring rolls in batches until golden, then drain on crumpled paper towel. Serve hot with the dipping sauce.

Dipping sauce

2 tablespoons soy sauce

1 tablespoon hoisin sauce

1 tablespoon plum sauce

1 tablespoon sweet chili sauce

34

Tortilla flutes

Makes
24

¼ cup olive oil

2 small onions, finely
  chopped

2 garlic cloves, crushed

½ teaspoon chili powder

2 teaspoons ground cumin

2 pounds 4 ounces cooked
  chicken meat, finely
  chopped

2 tablespoons finely chopped
  cilantro leaves

24 soft flour or corn tortillas

oil, for shallow-frying

red or green chili sauce,
  to serve

1 avocado, sliced, to serve

Heat the olive oil in a frying pan over medium heat and fry the onion and garlic for 2–3 minutes, or until the onion is just tender but not soft. Add the chili powder and cumin and stir for 1 minute. Add the chicken and mix well. Cook over medium heat until just heated through. Stir in the coriander and remove from the heat.

Soften the tortillas, one at a time, by heating in a dry heavy-based frying pan over high heat for about 30 seconds each side. Lay a tortilla flat on a work surface and place a large spoonful of chicken mixture along the center. Carefully roll up to form a flute.

Pour oil into a deep heavy-based frying pan to a depth of 2 inches and heat to 350°F, or until a cube of bread dropped into the oil turns golden brown in 15 seconds. Holding the flute together with tongs (or fasten with toothpicks), cook one at a time until slightly crisp. Drain on crumpled paper towel. Serve with chili sauce and avocado slices.

NOTE Speed up the preparation of this dish by buying a barbecued chicken and shredding the meat.

35

Makes
20

Vegetable bhaji

2 cups besan (chickpea flour)

I teaspoon chili powder

I teaspoon ground turmeric

¼ teaspoon asafoetida

I cup carrots, cut into thin
  sticks

I cup snow peas, cut into thin
  sticks

½ cup aubergine, cut into
  thin sticks

2—3 fresh curry leaves, very
  finely shredded

vegetable oil, for deep-frying

chutney or minted yogurt
  raita, to serve

Mix together the besan, chili powder, turmeric, asafoetida, and a pinch of salt. Add just enough cold water to make a thick batter, which will hold the vegetables together. Mix the vegetables and curry leaves into the batter.

Fill a deep-fryer or heavy-based saucepan one-third full with oil and heat to 350°F, or until a cube of bread dropped in the oil browns in 15 seconds. Lift clumps of vegetables out of the batter and lower carefully into the oil. Fry for 3—4 minutes, or until golden all over and cooked through, then drain on paper towel. Sprinkle with salt and serve hot with chutney or a minted yogurt raita.

NOTE The Indian ingredients for this dish, such as besan, asafoetida, and curry leaves, can be found in Asian grocery stores.

Serves
4

Burritos

1 pound rump steak

1 teaspoon olive oil

1 medium onion, finely
   sliced

1 cinnamon stick

4 cloves

1 bay leaf

2 cups beef stock

eight x 8 inch flour tortillas

tomato salsa, to serve

Trim meat of excess fat and cut into ¾ inch cubes. Heat the oil in a medium frying pan and add the onion. Cook over medium heat, stirring, until golden brown.

Add the meat, cinnamon stick, cloves, bay leaf, and beef stock. Bring to the boil. Reduce the heat and simmer, covered, for 30 minutes or until the meat is soft and almost all of the liquid has been absorbed. Remove and discard the cinnamon stick, cloves, and bay leaf.

Shred the meat with two forks. Serve rolled up in a tortilla with tomato salsa and salad.

NOTE The meat mixture will keep, covered, in the refrigerator for up to 4 days. Before serving, reheat it gently in a microwave oven or saucepan.

SOUPS
& MAINS
for hearty
EATERS

Serves 4

Perfect French onion soup

3 tablespoons butter

1 pound 10 ounces onions, finely sliced

2 garlic cloves, finely chopped

⅓ cup all-purpose flour

8 cups beef or chicken stock

1 cup white wine

1 dried bay leaf

2 thyme sprigs

8 slices of day-old baguette

1 cup shredded gruyère cheese

Melt the butter in a large, heavy-bottomed saucepan, then add the onions and cook over low heat for 25 minutes, stirring occasionally, or until the onions are golden and beginning to caramelize.

Add the garlic and flour and stir continuously for 2 minutes. Stirring, gradually add the stock and wine, then bring to the boil. Reduce the heat, add the bay leaf and thyme sprigs, then cover and simmer over medium–low heat for 25 minutes.

Remove the herbs, and season to taste. Preheat the broiler. Toast the baguette, divide among four warmed soup bowls, then ladle the soup over the top. Sprinkle with the grated cheese, then place the bowls under the broiler until the cheese melts and turns golden. Serve immediately.

NOTES French onion soup is far more complex in flavor than its few simple ingredients might suggest. Long, slow cooking gives the deep, savory flavors and silky texture that are characteristic of this soup. It's at its best when made with good, home-made brown beef stock.

1½ tablespoons coriander
  seeds

1 tablespoon cumin seeds

1 teaspoon ground turmeric

1 onion, roughly chopped

1 tablespoon ginger, roughly
  chopped

3 garlic cloves

3 lemon grass stems, white
  part only, sliced

6 macadamia nuts

4–6 small red chilies

3 teaspoons shrimp paste,
  roasted (see Note)

4 cups chicken stock

¼ cup oil

14 ounces chicken thigh
  fillets, cut into ¾-inch
  pieces

3 cups coconut milk

4 makrut (kaffir lime) leaves

2½ tablespoons lime juice

2 tablespoons fish sauce

2 tablespoons grated palm
  sugar (jaggery) or soft
  brown sugar

9 ounces dried rice
  vermicelli

1 cup bean sprouts, trimmed

4 fried tofu puffs, sliced
  thinly

3 tablespoons chopped
  Vietnamese mint

1 handful cilantro leaves

lime wedges, to serve

Serves
4–6

Chicken laksa

This spicy soup of chicken, noodles, and coconut milk is ultra-rich, but so satisfying that once you've tried it, only a big bowl will suffice.

Toast the coriander and cumin seeds in a frying pan over medium heat for 1–2 minutes, or until fragrant, tossing the pan constantly to prevent them from burning. Grind finely using a mortar and pestle or a spice grinder.

Put all the spices, the onion, ginger, garlic, lemon grass, macadamia nuts, chilies, and roasted shrimp paste in a food processor or blender. Add ½ cup of the stock and blend to a paste.

Heat the oil in a wok or large saucepan over low heat and gently cook the paste for 3–5 minutes, stirring constantly to prevent it from burning or sticking to the bottom of the pan. Add the remaining stock and bring to the boil over high heat. Reduce the heat to medium and simmer for 15 minutes, or until reduced slightly. Add the chicken and simmer for 4–5 minutes. Add the coconut milk, lime leaves, lime juice, fish sauce, and palm sugar, and simmer for 5 minutes over medium–low heat. Do not bring to the boil or cover with a lid, as the coconut milk will split.

Meanwhile, put the vermicelli in a heatproof bowl, cover with boiling water, and soak for 6–7 minutes, or until softened. Drain and divide among large serving bowls with the bean sprouts. Ladle the hot soup over the top and garnish with some tofu strips, mint, and coriander leaves. Serve with a wedge of lime.

Serves
4

Cream of chicken soup

¼ cup butter

¼ cup all-purpose flour

2 cups chicken stock

I cup milk

I cup whipping cream

I skinless, boneless chicken
  breast fillet, finely chopped

I celery stalk

fresh parsley, to serve

Melt the butter in a large pan, add the flour, and stir over low heat for 2 minutes, or until lightly golden. Remove from the heat and add the stock gradually, stirring until smooth. Return to the heat and stir until it comes to the boil and thickens. Add the milk, chicken, cream, and celery. Simmer for 5 minutes, or until the chicken and celery are tender. Season and sprinkle with parsley.

NOTES Cream of chicken soup can be served as is or puréed. If puréeing, allow it to cool for 15 minutes or so before processing it in a food processor or blender. Reheat gently to serve, without allowing the soup to boil.

As with all soups, you'll get the best results if you use home-made stock. Commercial stocks can be quite salty, so if you are using one of these, taste the soup just before serving and then add extra salt only if needed.

Serves
6

Shepherd's pie

3 tablespoons olive oil

1 large onion, finely chopped

2 garlic cloves, crushed

2 celery stalks, finely chopped

3 carrots, diced

2 bay leaves

1 tablespoon thyme, chopped

2 pounds ground lamb

1½ tablespoons all-purpose flour

½ cup dry red wine

2 tablespoons concentrated tomato purée

1½ cups tinned chopped tomatoes

1 pound 12 ounces potatoes, chopped

¼ cup milk

⅓ cup butter

½ teaspoon ground nutmeg

Heat 2 tablespoons of the oil in a large, heavy-based saucepan and cook the onion for 3–4 minutes, or until softened. Add the garlic, celery, carrot, bay leaves, and thyme, and cook for 2–3 minutes. Transfer to a bowl and remove the bay leaves.

Add the remaining oil to the same pan and cook the lamb over high heat for 5–6 minutes, or until it changes color. Mix in the flour, cook for 1 minute, then pour in the red wine and cook for 2–3 minutes. Return the vegetables to the pan with the tomato purée and tomato. Reduce the heat, cover, and simmer for 45 minutes, stirring occasionally. Season the mixture, if need be, and transfer it to a shallow 12 cup casserole dish. Preheat the oven to 350°F.

Boil the potatoes in salted water for 20–25 minutes, or until tender. Drain, then mash with the milk and butter until smooth. Season with nutmeg and black pepper. Spoon over the meat mixture and fluff with a fork. Bake for 40 minutes, until golden and crusty.

NOTE This dish can also be made wholly or partly with leftover roast lamb. Chop the lamb into chunks and pulse it in a food processor until ground. Cook it, along with raw ground lamb if you are using it, as described above.

Serves 4–6

41

Chili pork ribs

2 pounds pork
   spare ribs

½ cup puréed tomatoes

2 tablespoons honey

2 tablespoons chili sauce

2 tablespoons hoisin sauce

2 tablespoons lime juice

2 garlic cloves, crushed

1 tablespoon oil

Cut each rib into thirds, then lay the pieces in a single layer in a shallow non-metallic dish.

Mix together all the other ingredients except the oil and pour over the meat, turning to coat well. Cover with plastic wrap and refrigerate overnight, turning occasionally.

Drain the ribs, reserving the marinade, and cook them over medium heat on a lightly oiled barbecue grill plate or flat plate. Baste often with the reserved marinade and cook for 15–20 minutes, or until the ribs are tender and well browned, turning occasionally. Season to taste before serving immediately.

NOTES When choosing ribs, select those that have a high meat-to-fat ratio. Hoisin sauce is a Chinese dipping sauce made from sweet potato, wheat, or rice with various seasonings. It is especially common in Cantonese cooking.

Seafood terrine

First layer

1 pound uncooked shrimp, chilled

2 egg whites, chilled

pinch freshly grated nutmeg

1 cup pouring cream, chilled

1¼ cups baby green beans, trimmed

Second layer

9 ounces skinless salmon or ocean trout fillet, chopped

2 egg whites, chilled

2 tablespoons chopped chives

1 cup pouring cream, chilled

Preheat the oven to 350°F. Brush a 6-cup bar pan, measuring 4½ x 8½ inches, with oil and line the base with baking paper.

To make the first layer, peel the shrimp and gently pull out the dark vein from each shrimp back, starting at the head end. Finely chop the shrimp in a food processor. Add the egg whites one at a time, processing until smooth. Season with salt, pepper, and nutmeg. Gradually add the cream. Don't overprocess or it may curdle. Spoon into the prepared loaf pan, cover, and refrigerate.

Cook the beans in boiling water for 3 minutes, or until just tender, then drain and plunge into cold water. Drain and dry with paper towels. Arrange lengthways over the shrimp mixture.

To make the second layer, process the fish in a food processor until finely chopped. Add the egg whites one at a time and process until smooth. Add the chives. Gradually pour in the cream. Do not overprocess or it may curdle. Spread evenly over the beans.

Cover the terrine tightly with foil brushed with oil and put in a roasting pan. Pour cold water into the tray to come halfway up the side of the pan. Bake for 35 minutes, or until lightly set in the center. Cool before removing the foil. Cover with plastic wrap and refrigerate until firm. Serve at room temperature.

Meanwhile, to make the tomato coulis, score a cross in the base of each tomato. Put in a heatproof bowl and cover with boiling water. Leave for 30 seconds, then transfer to cold water, drain, and peel away the skin from the cross. Cut the tomatoes in half, scoop out and discard the seeds, and chop the flesh. Heat the oil in a saucepan, add the onion, and stir for 2–3 minutes, or until tender. Add the tomato and cook over medium heat, stirring often, for 8 minutes, or until reduced and thickened slightly. Stir in the Grand Marnier (if desired) and cook for 1 minute. Cool, then process in a food processor until smooth. Season to taste and serve with slices of terrine, garnished with watercress.

Tomato coulis

1 pound 10 ounces very ripe plum tomatoes

2 tablespoons extra virgin olive oil

1 onion, very finely chopped

2 tablespoons Grand Marnier (optional)

trimmed watercress, to garnish

Serves
4

Massaman beef curry

1 tablespoon tamarind pulp

½ cup boiling water

2 tablespoons oil

1 pound 10 ounces lean stewing beef, cubed

2 cups coconut milk

4 cardamom pods, bruised

2 cups coconut cream

2–3 tablespoons massaman curry paste

8 baby onions, peeled

8 new potatoes, peeled

2 tablespoons fish sauce

2 tablespoons palm sugar (jaggery)

⅔ cup unsalted peanuts, roasted and ground

cilantro leaves, to garnish

Place the tamarind pulp and boiling water in a bowl and set aside to cool. When cool, mash the pulp to dissolve it in the water, then strain and reserve the liquid. Discard the pulp.

Heat the oil in a wok or a large saucepan and cook the beef in batches over high heat for 5 minutes, or until browned. Reduce the heat, add the coconut milk and cardamom, and simmer for 1 hour, or until the beef is tender. Remove and reserve the beef. Strain and reserve the cooking liquid, discarding the solids.

Heat the coconut cream in the wok and stir in the curry paste. Cook for 5 minutes, or until the oil starts to separate from the cream.

Add the baby onions, potatoes, fish sauce, palm sugar, peanuts, beef mixture, reserved cooking liquid, and tamarind water, and simmer for 25–30 minutes. Garnish with cilantro leaves to serve.

NOTE Massaman curry is a mildly spiced, coconut-based curry from southern Thailand. It is most often made with beef and traditionally contains potatoes, and peanuts also. Tamarind pulp and massaman curry paste can be found in Asian grocery stores or larger supermarkets.

Beef wellington

44

Serves
6–8

- 2 pounds 12 ounces beef fillet or rib-eye in one piece
- 1 tablespoon oil
- 5 ounces pâté
- 2/3 cup sliced button mushrooms
- 13 ounce block puff pastry, thawed
- 1 egg, lightly beaten
- 1 sheet ready-rolled puff pastry, thawed

Preheat the oven to 415°F. Trim the meat of any excess fat and sinew. Fold the thinner part of the tail end under the meat and tie securely with kitchen twine at regular intervals to form an even shape.

Rub the meat with freshly ground black pepper. Heat the oil over high heat in a large frying pan. Add the meat and brown well all over. Remove from the heat and allow to cool. Remove the string.

Spread the pâté over the top and sides of the beef. Cover with the mushrooms, pressing them onto the pâté. Roll out the block of pastry on a lightly floured work surface to a rectangle large enough to completely enclose the beef.

Place the beef on the pastry, brush the edges with egg, and fold over to enclose the meat completely, brushing the edges of the pastry with the beaten egg to seal, and folding in the ends. Invert onto a greased cookie sheet so the seam is underneath. Cut leaf shapes from the sheet of puff pastry and use to decorate the wellington. Use the egg to stick on the shapes. Cut a few slits in the top to allow steam to escape. Brush the top and sides of the pastry with egg, and cook for 45 minutes for rare, 1 hour for medium, or 1½ hours for well done. Leave in a warm place for 10 minutes before cutting into slices for serving.

NOTE Use a firm pâté, discarding any jelly. Cover the pastry loosely with foil if it begins to darken too much.

45

Serves
4–6

Crisp-skin chicken with five-spice dipping salt

3 star anise

2 cinnamon sticks

1 piece dried tangerine
or orange peel

½ x ¾ inch piece of fresh
ginger, lightly smashed

½ cup dark soy sauce

/¼ cup light soy sauce

⅓ cup Chinese rice wine

¼ cup sugar

3 pound 8 ounce whole
chicken, rinsed, excess fat
removed from the cavity

8 cups oil, for deep-frying

cilantro sprigs, to garnish

In a large saucepan, combine the star anise, cinnamon, tangerine peel, ginger, soy sauces, rice wine, sugar, and 8 cups water. Stir over high heat to dissolve the sugar. Bring to the boil, then reduce to a simmer.

Add the chicken to the liquid, adding enough water to just cover the chicken. Simmer for 30 minutes, then remove from the heat and allow the chicken to rest in the liquid for 10 minutes. Carefully remove the chicken and put it on a wire rack over a plate for 3 hours in the fridge—do not cover the chicken or the skin won't dry properly. After 3 hours, the skin should feel like parchment.

To make the glaze, put the ingredients in a saucepan with ¾ cup water. Bring to the boil, then brush the mixture over the chicken using a pastry brush, making sure that you coat all of the skin thoroughly. Leave the chicken to dry on the rack in the fridge for another 2 hours.

Meanwhile, to make the dipping salt, heat a small wok or saucepan over low heat and add 1 tablespoon salt, the five-spice, peppercorns, and sugar. Dry-fry for 3–4 minutes, or until the peppercorns turn black and smell fragrant. Sift the mixture and discard the peppercorns.

Heat the oil in a large wok to 350°F, or until a piece of bread dropped in the oil browns in 15 seconds. Lower the chicken into the oil and deep-fry on one side until it is a rich, dark-brown color and very crisp. Carefully turn the chicken over and brown the other side. Remove the chicken and drain on paper towel. Sprinkle the skin with a little of the dipping salt and rest for 5 minutes.

To serve, use a cleaver to chop the chicken in half lengthways, then into bite-sized pieces. Garnish with coriander sprigs and serve with the dipping salt.

Glaze

¼ cup honey

2 tablespoons dark soy sauce

2 tablespoons Chinese black vinegar

Dipping salt

1 teaspoon Chinese five-spice powder

½ teaspoon sichuan peppercorns

1 teaspoon superfine sugar

46

Butter chicken

Serves
4–6

The naughtiness in this recipe is self-evident in the name. Butter, along with a generous amount of cream and yogurt, is what puts this dish firmly on the list of dietary misdeeds.

2 tablespoons peanut oil

2 pounds 4 ounces boneless, skinless chicken thighs, quartered

¼ cup butter or ghee

2 teaspoons garam masala

2 teaspoons sweet paprika

2 teaspoons ground coriander

I tablespoon grated fresh ginger

¼ teaspoon chili powder

I cinnamon stick

6 cardamom pods, bruised

I⅓ cups puréed tomatoes

I tablespoon sugar

¼ cup plain yogurt

½ cup whipping cream

I tablespoon lemon juice

steamed basmati rice and poppadoms, to serve

Heat a wok to very hot, add I tablespoon oil, and swirl to coat the base and side. Add half the chicken and stir-fry for about 4 minutes, or until nicely browned. Remove from the wok. Add a little extra oil, if needed, and brown the remaining chicken. Remove from the wok and set aside.

Reduce the heat to medium, add the butter, and stir until melted. Add the garam masala, paprika, coriander, ginger, chili powder, cinnamon stick, and cardamom pods, and stir-fry for I minute, or until the spices are fragrant. Return the chicken to the wok and mix in until coated in the spices. Add the puréed tomatoes and sugar, and simmer, stirring, for 15 minutes, or until the chicken is tender and the sauce is thick. Stir in the yogurt, cream, and lemon juice and simmer for 5 minutes, or until the sauce has thickened slightly. Serve with rice and poppadoms.

NOTE To bruise cardamom pods (or other herbs or spices), either put them on a mortar and crack or squash them slightly with a pestle, or place them on a chopping board and press down on them with the flat of a knife blade or a cleaver.

Barbecued chicken
with thai sticky rice

1 large chicken, cut into
    8–10 pieces

8 garlic cloves, chopped

6 cilantro roots, chopped

1 large handful cilantro
    leaves, chopped

1 tablespoon finely chopped
    fresh ginger

1 teaspoon ground white
    pepper

¼ cup fish sauce

¼ cup lime juice

¼ cup whiskey (optional)

3 cups long-grain glutinous
    rice

cucumber slices, to serve

Put the chicken pieces in a nonmetallic bowl. Combine the garlic, coriander root and leaves, ginger, white pepper, and a pinch of salt, and pound to a paste using a mortar and pestle. Mix in the fish sauce, lime juice, and whiskey (if using), then pour over the chicken and mix well. Marinate for at least 6 hours in the refrigerator. At the same time, soak the rice for at least 3 hours in cold water.

To make the sauce, pound the coriander root, garlic, chili, and a pinch of salt to a paste using a mortar and pestle, or process in a food processor. Combine the vinegar, sugar, and ¾ cup water in a saucepan and stir until the sugar has dissolved. Bring to the boil, then add the paste and cook for 8–10 minutes, or until reduced by half. Set aside until ready to serve.

Drain the rice well, then line a bamboo steamer with muslin or banana leaves, spread the rice over, and cover with a tight-fitting lid. Steam over a wok or large saucepan of boiling water for 40 minutes, or until the rice is translucent, sticky, and tender. If steam is escaping, wrap some foil over the top of the steamer. Keep covered until ready to serve.

Meanwhile, heat a barbecue to medium heat, then cook the chicken, turning regularly for about 25 minutes, or until tender and cooked through. The breast pieces may only take about 15 minutes, so take them off first and keep warm.

Serve the chicken, rice, dipping sauce, and cucumber on separate plates in the center of the table and allow your guests to help themselves.

Sauce

6 cilantro roots, chopped

4 garlic cloves, chopped

2 bird's eye chilies, seeded and chopped

¾ cup vinegar

4 tablespoons grated palm sugar (jaggery) or soft brown sugar

Serves
6

Chili con carne

1 tablespoon olive oil

1 brown onion, chopped

3 garlic cloves, crushed

2 tablespoons ground cumin

1½ teaspoons chili powder

1 pound 5 ounces ground beef

1⅔ cups canned crushed tomatoes

2 tablespoons concentrated tomato purée

2 teaspoons dried oregano

1 teaspoon dried thyme

2 cups beef stock

1 teaspoon sugar

1⅓ cups tinned red kidney beans, rinsed and drained

1 cup shredded cheddar cheese

½ cup sour cream

cilantro sprigs, to garnish

corn chips, to serve (optional)

With its combination of beans, beef, sour cream, and cheese, this dish packs a lot of energy into a small serve. Whether you're into robust outdoor activities or more languid indoor pastimes, a bowl of chili is an ideal fortifier.

Heat the oil in a large saucepan over medium heat, add the onion, and cook for 5 minutes, or until starting to brown. Add the garlic, cumin, chili powder, and ground beef, and cook, stirring, for 5 minutes, or until the beef has changed color. Break up any lumps with the back of a wooden spoon. Add the tomato, tomato paste, herbs, beef stock, and sugar, and stir to combine. Bring to the boil then reduce to a simmer and cook, stirring occasionally, for 1 hour, or until the sauce is rich and thick. Stir in the beans and cook for 2 minutes to heat through.

Divide the chili con carne among six serving bowls, sprinkle with the cheese, and top each with a tablespoon of the sour cream. Garnish with the coriander sprigs and serve with the corn chips if you wish.

47

Serves
6

Chicken kiev

½ cup butter, softened

1 clove garlic, crushed

2 tablespoons chopped fresh parsley

2 teaspoons lemon juice

2 teaspoons grated lemon zest

6 small chicken breasts, underbreast fillets removed

½ cup all-purpose flour

4 cups dried breadcrumbs

2 eggs, beaten

3 tablespoons milk

oil, for frying

lemon wedges, to serve

As well as being delicious on its own, chicken is a great carrier of other flavors. Here it encases a decadent herbed butter that permeates the meat and spurts forth when the roll is punctured by a fork. Have plenty of bread on hand for mopping up.

Mix together the butter, garlic, parsley, lemon juice, and zest. Spoon onto a sheet of foil and shape in a rectangle about 2 x 3 inches. Roll up the foil and chill until firm.

Place each piece of chicken between two sheets of plastic wrap and use a meat mallet or rolling pin to gently flatten it to about ¼ inch thick.

NOTE To make your own dried breadcrumbs, remove the crusts from slices of stale bread. Place the slices on cookie sheets in a single layer and cook in a low oven until crisp. Allow to cool then break into large chunks and process into crumbs in a food processor. Store in plastic bags in the freezer until needed. There is no need to thaw the crumbs before using.

Cut the chilled butter into six pieces. Place a piece in the center of each chicken slice, fold in the edges, and roll up to completely enclose. Fasten with toothpicks and refrigerate until firm.

Place the flour and breadcrumbs on separate plates or sheets of baking paper. Toss the chicken in the flour, dip in the combined egg and milk, and then coat with the breadcrumbs. Chill on a paper-lined tray in the fridge for 1 hour, then toss in the egg and breadcrumbs again. Half-fill a heavy-based frying pan with oil and cook the chicken in batches, for 5 minutes on each side, or until golden and cooked through. Drain on paper towel, remove the toothpicks and serve with lemon wedges.

50

Beef stroganoff

Serves 4

- 14 ounces beef fillet, cut into ½ x 2 inch strips
- 2 tablespoons all-purpose flour
- 3 tablespoons butter
- 1 onion, thinly sliced
- 1 garlic clove, crushed
- 9 ounces small Swiss brown mushrooms
- ¼ cup brandy
- 1 cup beef stock
- 1½ tablespoons concentrated tomato purée
- ¾ cup sour cream
- 1 tablespoon chopped flat-leaf parsley

Dust the beef strips in flour, shaking off any excess.

Melt half the butter in a large frying pan and cook the meat in small batches for 1–2 minutes, or until seared all over. Remove. Add the remaining butter to the pan and cook the onion and garlic over medium heat for 2–3 minutes, or until the onion softens. Add the mushrooms and cook for 2–3 minutes.

Pour in the brandy and simmer until nearly all of the liquid has evaporated, then stir in the stock and tomato purée. Cook for 5 minutes to reduce the liquid slightly. Return the beef strips to the pan with any juices and stir in the sour cream. Simmer for 1 minute, or until the sauce thickens slightly. Season with salt and freshly ground black pepper.

Garnish with the chopped parsley and serve immediately with fettucine or steamed rice.

Serves 4

Steak baguette
with onions and mustardy mayo

3 tablespoons olive oil, plus extra for frying

1 red onion, sliced

1 teaspoon soft brown sugar

2 teaspoons balsamic vinegar

1 teaspoon thyme leaves

1 tablespoon Dijon mustard

3 tablespoons mayonnaise

2 handfuls arugula

4 thin beef steaks

2 thick baguettes, cut in half, or 8 thick slices of good-quality bread

2 tomatoes, sliced

Heat 2 tablespoons of the oil in a saucepan. Add the onion and cook slowly, with the lid on, stirring occasionally, until the onion is soft but not brown. This could take up to 15 minutes. Remove the lid, add the sugar and vinegar, and cook for a further 10 minutes, or until the onion is soft and just browned. Take the pan off the stove and stir in the thyme.

Meanwhile, make the mustardy mayo by mixing together the mustard and mayonnaise in a small bowl. Drizzle the arugula with the remaining olive oil and season with salt and freshly ground black pepper.

Heat 1 tablespoon of the extra oil in a frying pan over high heat and cook the steaks for 2 minutes on each side, adding more oil if necessary. Season to taste. To serve, put out the bread, along with separate bowls containing the onion, mustardy mayo, arugula leaves, steak, and sliced tomatoes. Let everyone make their own baguette so they can get the perfect mix of all the flavors.

52

Serves
4

Beer-battered fish and wedges

3 large all-purpose potatoes

oil, for deep-frying

1 cup self-rising flour

1 egg, beaten

¾ cup beer

4 boneless white fish fillets

all-purpose flour,
   for dusting

½ cup tartar sauce, or
   mayonnaise mixed with
   1 tablespoon lemon juice

Wash the potatoes, but do not peel. Cut into thick wedges, then dry with paper towels. Fill a heavy-based saucepan two-thirds full with oil and heat to medium—hot. Gently lower the potato wedges into the oil and cook for 4 minutes, or until tender and lightly browned. Remove the wedges from the oil with a slotted spoon and drain on paper towels.

Sift the self-rising flour with some pepper into a large bowl and make a well in the center. Add the egg and beer. Using a wooden spoon, stir until just combined and smooth. Dust the fish fillets in the all-purpose flour, shaking off the excess. Add the fish fillets one at a time to the batter and toss until well coated. Remove the fish from the batter, draining off the excess.

Working with one piece of fish at a time, gently lower it into the medium—hot oil. Cook for 2 minutes, or until golden and crisp and cooked through. Carefully remove from the oil with a slotted spoon. Drain on paper towels, and keep the fish warm while you cook the remainder.

Return the potato wedges to the medium—hot oil. Cook for another 2 minutes, or until golden brown and crisp. Remove from the oil with a slotted spoon and drain on paper towels. Serve the wedges immediately with the fish, and tartar sauce or lemon mayonnaise.

NOTE Potatoes with yellow skin and flesh tend to be all-purpose varieties. Cultivars include Coliban, Yukon Gold, Katahdin, and Kennebec.

101 DISHES TO EAT BEFORE YOU DIE(t)

Serves 2

Scrambled eggs and salmon on brioche

4 fresh eggs

4 tablespoons cream

3 tablespoons unsalted butter

4½ ounces sliced smoked salmon

2 teaspoons finely chopped dill

2 individual brioche buns or 2 croissants

Although smoked salmon is not cheap, a little goes a long way and always makes a luxurious impression. It's hard to imagine a more decadent breakfast than this, and it's a great supper dish too, whether you want to dine alone in style or spoil someone special.

Crack the eggs into a bowl, add the cream, and beat well together. Season with some salt and black pepper.

Melt the butter in a nonstick frying pan. When it starts to sizzle, add the eggs and turn the heat down to low. Using a flat-ended wooden spoon, push the mixture around until it starts to set, then add the salmon and dill. Continue to cook, gently folding the salmon and dill through the mixture until the eggs are mostly cooked, and just a little liquid is left in the pan.

Cut the top off the brioche or croissants, scoop out some of the filling, then pile the scrambled eggs on top and serve.

54 · Serves 6

Classic burger with barbecue sauce

1 pound 10 ounces ground beef

9 ounces ground sausage

1 small onion, finely chopped

1 tablespoon Worcestershire sauce

2 tablespoons tomato ketchup

1 cup fresh breadcrumbs

1 egg, lightly beaten

2 large onions, extra, thinly sliced

6 whole-wheat rolls

6 small lettuce leaves

1 large tomato, sliced

Barbecue sauce

2 teaspoons oil

1 small onion, finely chopped

3 teaspoons brown vinegar

1 tablespoon soft brown sugar

4 tablespoons tomato ketchup

2 teaspoons Worcestershire sauce

2 teaspoons soy sauce

Place the ground beef and sausage in a large bowl. Add the onion, sauces, breadcrumbs, and egg. Mix thoroughly with your hands. Divide the mixture into six equal portions and shape into patties. Refrigerate for at least 30 minutes.

Place the patties on a hot, lightly oiled barbecue grill plate or flat plate. Barbecue over the hottest part of the fire for 8 minutes each side. Meanwhile, fry the extra onions on an oiled hotplate until golden. Alternatively, fry the meat and onions in separate large frying pans on the stovetop.

To make the barbecue sauce, heat the oil in a small saucepan. Cook the onion for 5 minutes, or until soft. Add the vinegar, sugar, and sauces, and stir until the sauce comes to the boil. Reduce the heat and simmer for 3 minutes. Allow to cool.

Split the rolls in half and fill each one with a lettuce leaf, meat patty, tomato slice, and fried onions. Top with a generous quantity of barbecue sauce.

STORAGE The burger patties can be prepared up to 4 hours in advance and stored, covered, in the refrigerator. The sauce can be made up to 1 week in advance. Store in the refrigerator.

Serves 6

Goulash soup with dumplings

2 pounds 4 ounces chuck steak

1 onion, finely chopped

1 garlic clove, crushed

2 tablespoons sweet paprika

pinch cayenne pepper

1 teaspoon caraway seeds

1²/₃ cups canned chopped tomatoes

3 cups chicken stock

12 ounces all-purpose potatoes, cut into ¾-inch cubes

1 green bell pepper, halved, seeded, and cut into thin strips

2 tablespoons sour cream

Dumplings

²/₃ cup self-rising flour

¼ cup finely grated parmesan cheese

2 teaspoons finely chopped thyme

1 egg, lightly beaten

This is the perfect dish for a slow cooker—you can just set it and forget it for a few hours, then make the dumplings at the last minute. The result is a one-pot wonder that will keep the winter chill at bay.

Trim the steak of any fat and cut it into ½-inch cubes. Put the steak, onion, garlic, paprika, cayenne pepper, caraway seeds, tomatoes, stock, and potato in a slow cooker. Cook on low for 4½ hours, or until the beef is tender and the potato is cooked through.

Stir in the bell pepper, then turn the slow cooker to high and cook for a further 1 hour with the lid off. Season to taste with salt and freshly ground black pepper.

To make the dumplings, put the flour and parmesan cheese in a bowl. Season with salt and stir in the thyme and egg. Transfer the mixture to a floured surface and lightly knead to a soft dough. Using 1 teaspoon of the mixture at a time, roll it into a ball. Drop the dumplings into the slow cooker. Cover and cook on high for 10—15 minutes, or until the dumplings are cooked through.

Gently lift the dumplings out of the slow cooker and divide among serving bowls. Stir the sour cream into the soup and ladle the soup over the dumplings.

56

Serves
4–6

2 pounds ground lamb

I onion, finely chopped

2 green chilies, finely
chopped

3 teaspoons grated fresh
ginger

3 garlic cloves, crushed

I teaspoon ground cardamom

I egg

⅓ cup fresh breadcrumbs

2 tablespoons ghee or oil

Sauce

I tablespoon ghee or oil

I onion, sliced

I green chili, finely chopped

3 teaspoons grated fresh
ginger

2 garlic cloves, crushed

I teaspoon ground turmeric

3 teaspoons ground
coriander

2 teaspoons ground cumin

I teaspoon chili powder

2 tablespoons white vinegar

¾ cup plain yogurt

I¼ cups coconut milk

steamed rice, to serve

Lamb kofta

Line a cookie sheet with baking paper. Place the minced
lamb in a large bowl. Add the onion, chili, ginger, garlic,
cardamom, egg, and breadcrumbs and season well. Mix
until combined. Roll level tablespoons of the mixture into
balls and place them on the prepared cookie sheet.

Heat the ghee in a frying pan, add the meatballs in two
batches, and cook over medium heat for 5 minutes, or until
browned all over. Transfer the meatballs to a large bowl.

To make the sauce, heat the ghee in the cleaned frying pan,
add the onion, chili, ginger, garlic, and turmeric, and
cook, stirring, over low heat until the onion is soft. Add
the coriander, cumin, chili powder, vinegar, meatballs,
and I⅓ cups water and stir gently. Cover and simmer for
30 minutes. Stir in the combined yogurt and coconut milk
and simmer for another IO minutes with the pan partially
covered. Serve with steamed rice.

NOTE Although this recipe
is Indian, various types of
koftas (dumplings or meatballs)
are found in many cuisines
throughout Central Asia, the
Middle East, and Africa.

Fritto misto di mare

9 ounces baby squid

12 large uncooked shrimp

8 small octopus

16 scallops, cleaned

12 fresh sardines, gutted and heads removed

9 ounces firm white fish fillets, skinned and cut into large cubes

Sauce

½ cup extra virgin olive oil

2 garlic cloves, crushed

3 anchovy fillets, finely minced

2 tablespoons finely chopped parsley

pinch of chili flakes

Batter

1⅔ cups all-purpose flour

⅓ cup olive oil

1 large egg white

oil, for deep-frying

lemon wedges, to serve

Preheat the oven to 275°F. Clean the squid by pulling the heads and tentacles out of the bodies along with any innards. Cut the heads off below the eyes, just leaving the tentacles. Discard the heads and set the tentacles aside. Rinse the bodies, pulling out the clear quills, and cut the bodies into rings. Peel and devein the shrimp, leaving the tails intact.

Clean the octopus by slitting the head and pulling out the inner parts. Cut out the eyes and hard beak, and rinse. If the octopus seem a bit big, cut them into halves or quarters.

To make the sauce, warm the oil in a frying pan. Add the garlic, anchovy, parsley, and chili flakes. Cook over low heat for 1 minute, or until the garlic is soft but not brown.

To make the batter, sift the flour and ¼ teaspoon salt into a bowl. Mix in the oil with a wooden spoon, then gradually add 1¼ cups tepid water, changing to a whisk when the mixture becomes liquid. Continue whisking until the batter is smooth and thick. Stiffly whisk the egg white and fold into the batter. Heat the oil in a deep-fat fryer or deep frying pan to 375°F, or until a piece of bread dropped into the oil becomes golden brown in 10 seconds.

Dry the seafood on paper towels so the batter will stick. Working with one type of seafood at a time, dip the pieces in batter. Shake off the excess batter, then carefully lower into the oil. Deep-fry for 2–3 minutes, depending on the size of the pieces. Drain on paper towels, then transfer to the oven. Do not crowd the seafood. Keep warm while you fry the remaining seafood. Serve the seafood immediately with lemon wedges and the sauce.

Serves 4

Chili chicken with tacos

1 tablespoon olive oil

1 onion, finely chopped

1 pound ground chicken

1–2 teaspoons mild chili powder

2 cups tinned chopped tomatoes

2 tablespoons concentrated tomato purée

1–2 teaspoons soft brown sugar

2 cups canned red kidney beans, drained and rinsed

taco shell, or corn chips, to serve

sour cream, to serve

Heat the oil in a large saucepan. Add the onion and cook over medium heat for 3 minutes, or until soft. Increase the heat to high and add the chicken. Cook until the chicken has browned, breaking up any lumps with a wooden spoon.

Add the chili powder to the chicken and cook for 1 minute. Stir in the tomato, tomato purée, and ½ cup water. Bring to the boil, then reduce the heat and simmer for 30 minutes. Stir through the sugar to taste and the kidney beans, then season if needed. Serve along with warmed corn chips or in taco shells with the sour cream.

NOTE The meat mixture can be made and frozen for 4 weeks in an airtight container. Taco shells also freeze well. They do not have to be thawed before reheating.

Serves
4

Glazed hoisin chicken stir-fry

½ teaspoon sesame oil

1 egg white

1 tablespoon cornstarch

1 pound 9 ounces boneless,
skinless chicken thighs,
cut into small cubes

2 tablespoons peanut oil

2 garlic cloves, chopped

1 tablespoon finely shredded
fresh ginger

1 tablespoon brown bean
sauce

1 tablespoon hoisin sauce

1 tablespoon Chinese rice
wine

1 teaspoon light soy sauce

4 scallions, finely sliced

steamed rice, to serve

Combine the sesame oil, egg white, and cornstarch in a
large nonmetallic bowl. Add the chicken, toss to coat in the
marinade, then cover with plastic wrap and marinate in the
refrigerator for at least 15 minutes.

Heat a wok over high heat, add the peanut oil, and swirl to
coat the base and side. Add the chicken in three batches and
stir-fry for 4 minutes at a time, or until cooked through.
Remove the chicken from the wok and set aside.

Reheat the wok over high heat, add a little extra oil if
necessary, then add the garlic and ginger and stir-fry for
1 minute. Return the chicken to the wok, add the bean sauce
and hoisin sauce, and cook, stirring, for 1 minute. Add the
rice wine, soy sauce, and scallion, and cook for 1 minute,
or until the sauce is thick and glossy and coats the chicken.
Serve with steamed rice.

Serves 4

Satay chicken

1 pound boneless, skinless chicken thighs

1 onion, roughly chopped

2 lemon grass stems, white part only, thinly sliced

4 garlic cloves

2 red chilies, chopped

2 teaspoons ground coriander

1 teaspoon ground cumin

1 tablespoon soy sauce

¼ cup oil, or as needed

1 tablespoon soft brown sugar

cucumber slices and chopped roasted peanuts, to garnish

Peanut sauce

½ cup crunchy peanut butter

1 cup coconut milk

1–2 tablespoons sweet chili sauce

1 tablespoon soy sauce

2 teaspoons lemon juice

Soak 20 wooden skewers in cold water for 30 minutes to prevent scorching. Cut the chicken into 20 thick flat strips and thread onto the skewers.

Mix the onion, lemon grass, garlic, chili, coriander, cumin, soy sauce, and ½ teaspoon salt in a food processor until smooth, adding a little oil if necessary. Spread the mixture over the chicken, cover, and refrigerate for 30 minutes.

To make the peanut sauce, combine all the ingredients with ½ cup water over low heat and stir until the mixture boils. Remove from the heat. The sauce will thicken on standing.

Brush a very hot chargrill pan or barbecue flat plate with the remaining oil. Cook the skewers in batches for 2–3 minutes on each side, sprinkling with a little oil and brown sugar. Serve with the peanut sauce, cucumber slices, and chopped peanuts, if desired.

Lamb korma

One 4 pound 8 ounce leg
 of lamb, boned

1 onion, chopped

2 teaspoons grated fresh
 ginger

3 garlic cloves

1 tablespoon coriander seeds

2 teaspoons ground cumin

1 teaspoon cardamom pods

large pinch cayenne pepper

2 tablespoons ghee or oil

1 onion, extra, sliced

2 tablespoons concentrated
 tomato purée

½ cup plain yogurt

sliced scallions, to garnish

steamed rice, to serve

Remove all excess fat, skin, and sinew from the lamb. Cut the meat into 1¼ inch cubes and put in a large bowl.

Process the onion, ginger, garlic, coriander seeds, cumin, cardamom pods, cayenne pepper, and ½ teaspoon salt in a food processor until the mixture forms a smooth paste. Add a little water if needed. Add the spice mixture to the lamb, mix well to coat, and set aside for 1 hour.

Heat the ghee in a large frying pan. Add the extra onion and cook, stirring, over medium–low heat until the onion is soft. Add the lamb mixture and cook for 8–10 minutes, stirring constantly, until the lamb cubes are browned all over. Add the tomato purée and 2 tablespoons of the yogurt, and stir until combined. Simmer, uncovered, until the liquid has been absorbed. Add the remaining yogurt, 2 tablespoons at a time, stirring until the mixture is nearly dry between each addition. Cover the pan and simmer over low heat for 30 minutes, or until the meat is tender, stirring occasionally. Add a little water if the mixture becomes too dry. Garnish with scallions and serve with steamed rice.

62

Serves
4

Pizza crust

1 sachet dry yeast

½ teaspoon salt

½ teaspoon sugar

2½ cups all-purpose flour

2 tablespoons olive oil

2 teaspoons semolina
   or cornmeal

Topping

3 tablespoons pizza sauce

1 cup grated mozzarella
   cheese

1 green bell pepper, chopped

heaping 1 cup sliced small
   button mushrooms

⅓ cup sliced ham, cut into
   strips

⅓ cup thinly sliced kabanosy

¼ cup sliced salami, cut into
   quarters

2 pineapple rings, sliced

pitted black olives, sliced

Pizza supreme

Combine the yeast, salt, sugar, and 1 cup warm water in a small bowl. Leave, covered with plastic wrap for 10 minutes, or until the mixture is foamy.

Sift the flour into a large bowl. Make a well in the center, add the yeast mixture, and mix to a dough. If you like a thick pizza base, use all the dough; otherwise, for a thin base, use half and freeze the rest for another time.

Knead the dough on a lightly floured surface for 5 minutes, or until smooth and elastic. Roll the dough out to a 14-inch round. Preheat the oven to 415°F.

Brush a 12-inch round pizza tray with oil and sprinkle with semolina or cornmeal. Place the dough on the tray and tuck the edge underneath to make a rim. Spread pizza sauce on the base. Sprinkle most of the cheese over the base. Top with bell pepper and mushrooms. Arrange the ham, kabanosy, salami, pineapple, and olives evenly over the top. Sprinkle with the remaining cheese.

Bake for 30 minutes, or until the crust is crunchy and the cheese has melted. Cut into wedges to serve.

NOTE For a whole-wheat pizza crust, use 1½ cups all-purpose flour and 1 cup all-purpose whole-wheat flour.

Roast beef with Yorkshire puddings

Serves
6

one piece roasting beef
   (scotch fillet, rump, or
   sirloin), about 4 pounds
   8 ounces
2 garlic cloves, crushed

Yorkshire puddings
¾ cup all-purpose flour
½ cup milk
2 eggs

Red wine gravy
2 tablespoons all-purpose
   flour
⅓ cup red wine
2⅓ cups beef stock

Preheat the oven to 475°F. Rub the beef with the garlic and freshly cracked black pepper and drizzle with oil. Bake on a rack in a roasting pan for 20 minutes.

To make the Yorkshire puddings, sift the flour and ½ teaspoon salt into a large bowl, then whisk in the milk. In a separate bowl, whisk the eggs together until fluffy, then add to the batter and mix well. Add ½ cup water and whisk until large bubbles form on the surface. Cover the bowl with plastic wrap and refrigerate for 1 hour.

Reduce the oven to 350°F and continue to roast the meat for 1 hour for rare, or longer for well done. Cover loosely with foil and leave in a warm place while cooking the Yorkshire puddings.

Increase the oven to 425°F. Pour the pan juices into a pitcher and spoon ½ teaspoon into each of twelve patty or muffin pans. (Reserve the remaining juice for the gravy.) Heat the muffin pans in the oven until the fat is almost smoking. Whisk the batter again until bubbles form on the surface. Fill each muffin pan to three-quarters full. Bake for 20 minutes, or until puffed and lightly golden.

Meanwhile, to make the gravy, heat 2 tablespoons of pan juices in the roasting pan on the stovetop over low heat. Add the flour and stir well. Cook over medium heat for 1–2 minutes, stirring constantly, until the flour is well browned. Off the heat, gradually stir in the wine and stock. Return to the heat, stirring constantly, until the gravy boils and thickens. Simmer for 3 minutes, then season to taste with salt and pepper. Strain, if desired. Serve the beef with the hot Yorkshire puddings and red wine gravy.

64

Quiche lorraine

Pastry

1¾ cups all-purpose flour

heaping ⅓ cup chilled
butter, chopped

2 tablespoons iced water

Filling

2 tablespoons butter

1 onion, finely chopped

3 bacon slices, finely chopped

3 eggs

¾ cup whipping cream

1 cup grated gruyère cheese

¼ teaspoon freshly grated
nutmeg

To make the pastry, sift the flour into a bowl, add the chilled butter, and rub it into the flour with your fingertips until the mixture resembles fine breadcrumbs. Make a well in the center and add the iced water. Mix with a flat-bladed knife, using a cutting action, until the mixture comes together in beads. Add a little more water if needed. Turn out onto a lightly floured surface and gather into a ball. Cover with plastic wrap and refrigerate for 20 minutes.

Preheat the oven to 375°F. Roll out the pastry between two sheets of baking paper to fit a shallow, loose-based, 10-inch tart pan. Lift the pastry into the pan and press it well into the sides. Trim off any excess by rolling a rolling pin across the top of the pan. Refrigerate the pastry for 20 minutes. Cover the shell with baking paper, fill evenly with baking beads or uncooked rice, and bake for 15 minutes, or until the pastry is dried out and golden. Cool slightly before filling. Reduce the oven temperature to 350°F.

To make the filling, melt the butter in a frying pan and cook the onion and bacon over medium heat for 10 minutes. Cool, then spread over the cooled pastry.

Whisk together the eggs, cream, and half of the gruyère cheese and season to taste. Pour over the onion and sprinkle with the remaining gruyère and the nutmeg. Bake for 30 minutes, or until just firm. Serve warm or at room temperature.

Soups & Mains for Hearty Eaters

Serves
4

Shish kebabs with bell peppers and herbs

one 2 pound 4 ounce
    boneless leg of lamb

1 red bell pepper

1 green bell pepper

3 red onions

Marinade

1 onion, thinly sliced

2 garlic cloves, crushed

¼ cup lemon juice

⅓ cup olive oil

1 tablespoon chopped thyme

1 tablespoon paprika

½ teaspoon chili flakes

2 teaspoons ground cumin

¼ cup flat-leaf parsley

¼ cup chopped mint

bread or rice, to serve

Trim the sinew and most of the fat from the lamb and cut the meat into 1¼-inch cubes. Mix all the ingredients for the marinade in a large bowl. Season well, add the meat, and mix well. Cover and refrigerate for 4–6 hours, or overnight.

Remove the seeds and membrane from the peppers and cut the flesh into 1¼ inch-squares. Cut each red onion into six wedges. Remove the lamb from the marinade and reserve the liquid. Thread the meat onto the skewers, alternating them with the onion and pepper pieces. Broil the skewers for 5–6 minutes, brushing frequently with the marinade for the first couple of minutes. Serve immediately, with bread or rice.

NOTE If you're using wooden skewers, soak them first in cold water for about 20 minutes to prevent them from burning. Metal skewers can be oiled to prevent the meat from sticking to them.

Serves
6–8

Roast turkey
with country sage stuffing

One 6 pound 12 ounce turkey

2 tablespoons oil

2 cups chicken stock

2 tablespoons all-purpose
flour

Country sage stuffing

3 tablespoons butter

1 onion, finely chopped

1 celery stick, sliced

10 large sage leaves, shredded

2 cups fresh white
breadcrumbs

1½ teaspoons dried sage

4 tablespoons finely chopped
flat-leaf parsley

2 egg whites, lightly beaten

1 teaspoon salt

½ teaspoon white pepper

Celebrations such as Christmas and Thanksgiving call for indulgent food. A tender roasted bird makes a welcome centerpiece for any festive table.

Remove the neck and giblets from inside the turkey. Wash the turkey well and pat dry inside and out with paper towels. Preheat the oven to 350°F.

To make the stuffing, melt the butter in a small saucepan and cook the onion and celery over medium heat for 3 minutes, or until the onion has softened. Transfer to a bowl and add the sage leaves, breadcrumbs, dried sage, parsley, egg whites, salt, and white pepper. Loosely stuff this mixture into the turkey cavity. Tuck the wings underneath and close the cavity with a skewer. Tie the legs together. Place on a rack in a roasting pan. Roast for 2 hours, basting with the combined oil and ½ cup of the stock. Cover the breast and legs with foil after 1 hour if the turkey is overbrowning. Remove from the oven, cover, and leave to rest for 15 minutes.

To make the gravy, drain off all but 2 tablespoons of pan juices from the roasting pan. Place the dish on the stove over low heat, add the flour, and stir well. Stir over medium heat until browned. Gradually add the remaining stock, stirring until the gravy boils and thickens. Serve the turkey with the gravy and roast vegetables.

Serves
4

Sweet and sour pork

Place the pork in a shallow glass or ceramic bowl. Combine the cornstarch with the sherry, soy sauce, and half the sugar, and pour into the bowl. Cover and refrigerate for 30 minutes.

Drain the pork, reserving the marinade. Heat the wok until very hot, add 2 tablespoons of the oil, and swirl to coat the side. Stir-fry half of the pork over high heat for 4—5 minutes, or until golden brown and just cooked. Remove from the wok, add more oil if necessary, and repeat with the remaining pork. Remove all the pork from the wok.

Reheat the wok, add 1 tablespoon of oil, and stir-fry the onion over high heat for 3—4 minutes, or until slightly softened. Add the pepper and carrot, and cook for 3—4 minutes, or until tender. Stir in the marinade, cucumber, scallions, pineapple, vinegar, ½ teaspoon salt, the remaining sugar, and ⅓ cup of the pineapple juice.

Bring to the boil and simmer for 2—3 minutes, or until the sauce has thickened slightly. Return the pork to the wok and toss to heat through, then serve at once with steamed rice.

1 pound pork fillet, cut into thick slices

2 tablespoons cornstarch

1 tablespoon sherry

1 tablespoon soy sauce

1 tablespoon sugar

oil, for cooking

1 large onion, thinly sliced

1 green bell pepper, cut into squares

2 small carrots, thinly sliced

1 small short cucumber, seeded and chopped

5 scallions, cut into short lengths

15½ ounces canned pineapple pieces in natural juice, drained and juice reserved

¼ cup white vinegar

steamed rice, to serve

68

Serves
6

Sesame tempura shrimp

Soy dipping sauce

1 tablespoon grated fresh ginger

1 cup Japanese soy sauce

1 tablespoon sesame seeds, toasted

1 tablespoon superfine sugar

oil, for deep-frying

1 cup tempura flour

2 tablespoons sesame seeds

1 pound 10 ounces uncooked shrimp, peeled and deveined, tails left intact

Combine the soy dipping sauce ingredients in a small bowl.

Fill a deep, heavy-based saucepan one-third full of oil and heat to 350°F, or until a cube of bread dropped in the oil browns in 15 seconds. Place the tempura flour and the sesame seeds in a bowl and gradually stir in ¾ cup iced water with chopsticks until just combined. (The batter should still be lumpy.)

Dip the shrimp, 3–4 at a time, into the batter and deep-fry for 1–2 minutes, or until golden brown. Drain on crumpled paper towel and serve at once with the sauce.

NOTES For a crisp tempura batter, be sure to use iced water, and stir the mixture just until combined; there should still be a few lumps of flour.

Soy sauce is available in regular and low-salt varieties; use whichever you prefer in this dish.

69

Serves
8

Pork with apple and prune stuffing

1 green apple, chopped

⅓ cup pitted prunes, chopped

2 tablespoons port

1 tablespoon chopped flat-leaf parsley

4 pound 8 ounce piece boned pork loin

olive oil and salt, to rub on the pork

Wine gravy

2 tablespoons all-purpose flour

2 teaspoons Worcestershire sauce

2 tablespoons red or white wine

2¼ cups beef or chicken stock

Preheat the oven to 475°F. To make the stuffing, combine the apple, prunes, port, and parsley. Lay the pork loin on a board with the rind underneath. Spread the stuffing over the meat side of the loin, roll up, and secure with skewers or string at regular intervals. If some of the filling falls out while tying, carefully push it back in. Score the pork rind with a sharp knife at ½-inch intervals (if the butcher hasn't already done so) and rub generously with oil and salt.

Place the pork on a rack in a roasting pan. Bake for 15 minutes, then reduce the heat to 350°F and bake for a further 1½–2 hours, or until the pork is cooked through. The juices will run clear when a skewer is inserted into the thickest part of the meat. Cover and stand for 15 minutes before removing the skewers or string and carving. Reserve any pan juices for making the gravy.

To make the gravy, discard all but 2 tablespoons of the pan juices from the roasting pan. Heat the dish on the stovetop over medium heat, stir in the flour, and cook, stirring, until well browned. Remove from the heat and gradually add the Worcestershire sauce, wine, and stock. Return to the heat. Stir until the mixture boils and thickens, then simmer for 2 minutes. Season with salt and pepper, to taste.

Moussaka

2 large tomatoes

3 pounds 5 ounces aubergine, cut into ¼-inch slices

½ cup olive oil

2 onions, finely chopped

2 large garlic cloves, crushed

½ teaspoon ground allspice

1 teaspoon ground cinnamon

1 pound 10 ounces ground lamb

2 tablespoons concentrated tomato purée

½ cup dry white wine

3 tablespoons chopped flat-leaf parsley

Score a cross in the base of each tomato. Put in a heatproof bowl and cover with boiling water. Leave for 30 seconds, then transfer to cold water and peel the skin away from the cross. Cut each tomato in half, scoop out the seeds, and finely chop the flesh. Lay the aubergine on a tray, sprinkle with salt, and leave for 30 minutes. Rinse and pat dry.

Heat 2 tablespoons of the olive oil in a frying pan, add the aubergine in batches, and cook for 1–2 minutes each side, or until golden and soft. Add a little more oil when needed. Heat 1 tablespoon of the olive oil in a large saucepan, add the onion, and cook over medium heat for 5 minutes. Add the garlic, allspice, and cinnamon, and cook for 30 seconds. Add the lamb and cook for 5 minutes, or until browned, breaking up any lumps with the back of a spoon. Add the tomato, tomato purée, and wine, and simmer over low heat for 30 minutes, or until the liquid has evaporated. Stir in the chopped parsley and season to taste with salt and black pepper. Preheat the oven to 350°F.

To make the cheese sauce, melt the butter in a saucepan over low heat. Stir in the flour and cook for 1 minute, or until pale and foaming. Remove the saucepan from the heat and gradually stir in the milk and nutmeg. Return the saucepan to the heat and stir constantly until the sauce boils and thickens. Reduce the heat and simmer for 2 minutes. Stir in 1 tablespoon of the cheese until well combined.

Line the base of a 12-cup ovenproof dish, measuring 10 x 12 inches, with one-third of the aubergine. Spoon half the meat sauce over it and cover with another layer

of aubergine. Spoon the remaining meat sauce over the top and cover with the remaining aubergine. Stir the egg into the cheese sauce. Spread the sauce over the top of the aubergine and sprinkle with the remaining cheese. Bake for 1 hour. Leave to stand for 10 minutes before slicing.

NOTE You can substitute an equal quantity of sliced, pan-fried zucchini or potatoes, or any combination of these vegetables, for the aubergine.

Cheese sauce

¼ cup butter

½ cup all-purpose flour

2½ cups milk

pinch freshly grated nutmeg

⅓ cup freshly grated kefalotyri or parmesan cheese

2 eggs, lightly beaten

71

Serves
4

Veal schnitzel

4 thin veal steaks

all-purpose flour,
    for coating

1 egg, lightly beaten

1 cup dried breadcrumbs

¼ cup oil

2 tablespoons butter

1 lemon, cut into wedges

2 tablespoons capers

2 pickled cucumbers, sliced

Trim the meat of any fat and sinew. Place it between two sheets of plastic wrap and flatten with a meat mallet or a rolling pin to ¼ inch thick. Nick the edges to prevent them from curling when the steaks are cooked. Pat dry with paper towel.

Season the flour with salt and black pepper. Coat the veal with the seasoned flour, shaking off the excess. Dip into the egg and then coat in breadcrumbs. Place on a foil-lined tray. Cover and refrigerate for at least 30 minutes to firm up the breadcrumb coating.

Heat the oil and butter in a large heavy-based pan and cook the veal over medium heat for 3–4 minutes. Turn over and cook for 2–3 minutes, or until golden. Serve at once with lemon, capers, and pickled cucumbers.

NOTE The schnitzels can be coated with breadcrumbs several hours in advance. Keep them covered and refrigerated until ready to fry.

VARIATION Prepare chicken schnitzel in the same way. Use boneless, skinless chicken breasts and flatten with a meat mallet before cooking.

Serves 4

Eggs benedict

Hollandaise sauce

¾ cup butter

4 egg yolk

1 teaspoon tarragon vinegar

2 tablespoons lemon juice

8 eggs, straight from the fridge

8 slices prosciutto or bacon

4 English muffins, split

Why not start the day as you mean to go on—indulgently—with soft-poached eggs with an unctuous buttery sauce sharpened with lemon juice? If you can persuade someone to serve you this dish as part of a breakfast in bed, so much the better.

To make the hollandaise sauce, melt the butter in a small saucepan. Place the egg yolks, 2 tablespoons water, the tarragon vinegar and the lemon juice in a food processor and, with the motor running, gradually add the butter. Process until the mixture is thick and creamy.

Turn on the broiler. Put a large frying pan full of water over high heat. When the water is bubbling, turn the heat down to a simmer. Crack an egg into a cup and slip the egg into the water. The egg should start to turn opaque as it hits the water. Do the same with 7 more eggs, keeping them separated. Turn the heat down and leave the eggs for 3 minutes.

NOTE Hollandaise sauce is usually cooked, which can cause the eggs to curdle. This easy uncooked version avoids that problem and is just as delicious. It will warm slightly on contact with the hot eggs.

154

Put the prosciutto or bacon on a cookie sheet, place it under the broiler for 2 minutes, then turn it over and cook the other side. Put the muffins in a toaster or under the grill to toast.

Put the muffins on plates and put a slice of prosciutto on each. Lift each egg out of the water, drain, and put them on top of the prosciutto. Spoon some hollandaise sauce over each egg.

VARIATION Slices of smoked salmon can be used instead of the ham.

PASTA, RICE, & Noodles

Vietnamese fried rice

¼ cup fish sauce

2 tablespoons soy sauce

2 teaspoons sugar

3 eggs

½ cup oil

1 large onion, finely chopped

6 scallions, chopped

4 garlic cloves, finely
  chopped

2 inch piece fresh ginger,
  grated

2 small red chilies, seeded
  and finely chopped

9 ounces pork loin fillet,
  finely chopped

4½ ounces Chinese sausage
  (lap cheong), thinly sliced

¾ cup chopped green beans

⅔ cup chopped carrots

½ large red bell pepper,
  seeded, membrane
  removed and chopped

2½ cups cold, cooked jasmine
  rice

Combine the fish sauce, soy sauce, and sugar in a bowl, stirring until the sugar dissolves. Set aside until needed.

Whisk the eggs and ¼ teaspoon salt together. Heat 1 tablespoon of the oil in a wok and swirl the oil to coat the base and side. Pour in the egg and cook over medium heat, stirring regularly, for 2–3 minutes, or until just cooked. Remove from the wok.

Heat another tablespoon of oil in the wok and stir-fry the onion, scallion, garlic, ginger, and chili for 7 minutes, or until the onion is soft, then remove from the wok. Add a little more oil and stir-fry the pork and sausage for 3–4 minutes, then remove and set aside.

Add the rest of the oil and stir-fry the beans, carrot, and pepper for 1 minute, then add the rice and cook for 2 minutes. Return everything except the egg to the wok, add the fish sauce mixture, and toss. Add the egg, toss lightly to combine, and serve.

74

Serves
8

2 tablespoons olive oil

4 garlic cloves, crushed

3 onions, chopped

2 pounds 4 ounces ground lamb

3¼ cups canned chopped tomatoes

1 cup dry red wine

1 cup chicken stock

3 tablespoons concentrated tomato purée

2 tablespoons oregano leaves

2 bay leaves

12 ounces ziti or spaghetti

2 eggs, lightly beaten

3 cups Greek-style yogurt

3 eggs, extra, lightly beaten

7 ounces kefalotyri or manchego cheese, grated (see Note)

½ teaspoon ground nutmeg

½ cup grated parmesan cheese

1 cup fresh breadcrumbs

Pastitsio

Preheat the oven to 400°F. To make the meat sauce, heat the oil in a large, heavy-based saucepan and cook the garlic and onion over low heat for 10 minutes, or until the onion is soft and golden.

Add the lamb and cook over high heat until browned, stirring constantly and breaking up any lumps with a wooden spoon. Add the tomato, wine, stock, tomato purée, oregano, and bay leaves. Bring to the boil, reduce the heat, and simmer, covered, for 15 minutes. Remove the lid and cook for 30 minutes. Season with salt and pepper.

While the meat is cooking, cook the pasta in a large saucepan of rapidly boiling salted water until al dente. Drain well. Transfer to a bowl and stir the eggs through. Spoon into a lightly greased 16-cup ovenproof dish. Top with the meat sauce.

Whisk the yogurt, extra eggs, cheese, and nutmeg in a bowl to combine, and pour the mixture over the meat sauce. Sprinkle with the combined parmesan cheese and breadcrumbs. Bake for 30–35 minutes, or until the top of the pastitsio is crisp and golden. Leave for 20 minutes before slicing.

NOTE Kefalotyri and manchego are firm, grating cheeses. Use parmesan if they are unavailable.

Pasta, Rice, & Noodles

75

Potato gnocchi

Gnocchi

2 pounds 4 ounces floury
   potatoes, unpeeled

2 egg yolks, lightly beaten

2 tablespoons grated
   parmesan cheese

1½ cups all-purpose flour,
   plus extra for kneading

Sauce

1 tablespoon butter

½ cup pancetta or bacon
   slices, cut into thin strips

8 very small sage or basil
   leaves

scant ⅔ cup heavy cream

½ cup shaved parmesan
   cheese

Prick the potatoes all over, then bake for 1 hour, or until tender. Leave to cool for 15 minutes, then peel and mash, or put through a potato ricer or a mouli (do not use a blender or food processor).

Mix in the egg yolks and parmesan cheese, then gradually stir in the flour. When the mixture gets too firm to use a spoon, work with your hands. Once a loose dough forms, transfer to a lightly-floured surface and knead gently. Work in enough extra flour to give a soft, pliable dough that is damp to the touch but not sticky.

Divide the dough into six portions. Working with one portion at a time, roll out on the floured surface to make a rope about ⅝ inch thick. Cut the rope into ⅝-inch lengths. Take one piece of dough and press your finger into it to form a concave shape, then roll the outer surface over the tines of a fork to make deep ridges. Fold the outer lips in towards each other to make a hollow in the middle. Set aside and continue with the remaining dough.

Bring a large saucepan of salted water to the boil. Add the gnocchi in batches, about 20 at a time. Stir gently and cook for 1–2 minutes, or until they rise to the surface. Remove with a slotted spoon, drain, and put the gnocchi in a greased shallow casserole dish or baking tray.

Meanwhile, preheat the oven to 400°F. To make the sauce, melt the butter in a frying pan and fry the pancetta until crisp. Stir in the sage leaves and cream. Season with sea salt and freshly ground black pepper and simmer for 10 minutes, or until thickened.

Pour the sauce over the gnocchi, toss gently, and sprinkle the parmesan on top. Bake for 10–15 minutes, or until the parmesan cheese melts and turns golden. Serve hot.

Serves
6

Spaghetti carbonara

1 pound spaghetti

8 bacon slices

4 eggs

½ cup freshly grated
   parmesan cheese

1¼ cups pouring cream

chopped chives, to garnish

Cook the spaghetti in a large saucepan of rapidly boiling salted water until al dente. Drain and return to the pan.

While the pasta is cooking, discard the bacon rind and cut the bacon into thin strips. Cook in a heavy-based frying pan over medium heat until crisp. Remove and drain on paper towels.

Beat the eggs, parmesan, and cream in a bowl until well combined. Add the bacon and pour the sauce over the warm pasta. Toss gently until the pasta is well coated.

Return the pan to the heat and cook over low heat for 1 minute, or until the sauce is slightly thickened. Season with freshly ground black pepper and serve garnished with chopped chives.

NOTE Although spaghetti is the traditional pasta for this dish, any other long pasta, such as linguine or fettucine, will also work.

Serves 6

Chicken and chorizo paella

¼ teaspoon saffron threads

¼ cup olive oil

I large red bell pepper, seeded and cut into ¼-inch strips

I pound 5 ounces boneless, skinless chicken thighs, cut into 1¼-inch cubes

7 ounces chorizo sausage, cut into ¾-inch slices

2 cups thinly sliced mushrooms

3 garlic cloves, crushed

I tablespoon finely grated lemon zest

3½ cups roughly chopped ripe tomatoes

1⅔ cups green beans, cut into 1¼-inch lengths

I tablespoon chopped rosemary

2 tablespoons chopped flat-leaf parsley

2 cups short-grain rice

3 cups hot chicken stock

lemon wedges, to serve

If carbohydrates are your downfall, any dish containing this much rice should result in some serious backsliding. True paella fans particularly value the crisp, caramelized crust that forms on the bottom of the pan.

Put the saffron in a bowl and pour over ¼ cup hot water. Set aside to infuse.

Heat the olive oil in a paella pan or in a large, deep, heavy-based frying pan over medium heat. Add the pepper and cook, stirring, for about 6 minutes, or until softened, then remove from the pan.

Add the chicken to the pan and cook for 10 minutes, or until brown all over. Remove from the pan. Add the chorizo and cook for 5 minutes, or until golden all over. Remove from the pan. Add the mushrooms, garlic, and lemon zest and cook for 5 minutes. Stir in the tomato and pepper and cook for another 5 minutes, or until the tomato is soft.

Add the beans, rosemary, parsley, saffron mixture, rice, chicken, and chorizo. Stir briefly and then add the hot stock. Do not stir from now on. Reduce the heat to low and simmer for 30 minutes. Remove from the heat, cover, and leave to stand for 10 minutes. Serve with lemon wedges.

Creamy seafood ravioli

Pasta

2 cups all-purpose flour

3 eggs

1 tablespoon olive oil

1 egg yolk, extra

Filling

3 tablespoons butter, softened

3 garlic cloves, finely chopped

2 tablespoons finely chopped flat-leaf parsley

3½ ounces scallops, cleaned and finely chopped

3½ ounces raw shrimp meat, finely chopped

To make the pasta, sift the flour and a pinch of salt into a bowl and make a well in the centre. Whisk the eggs, oil, and 1 tablespoon water in a bowl, then add gradually to the flour and mix to a firm dough. Gather into a ball.

Knead on a lightly floured surface for 5 minutes, or until smooth and elastic. Transfer to a lightly oiled bowl, cover with plastic wrap, and set aside for 30 minutes.

To make the filling, mix together the softened butter, garlic, parsley, scallops, and shrimp meat. Set aside.

Roll out a quarter of the pasta dough at a time until very thin (each portion of dough should be roughly 4 inches wide when rolled). Place 1 teaspoonful of filling at 2-inch intervals down one side of each strip. Whisk the extra egg yolk with ¼ cup water. Brush along one side of the dough and between the filling. Fold the dough over the filling to meet the other side. Repeat with the remaining filling and dough. Press the edges of the dough together firmly to seal.

Cut between the mounds with a knife or a fluted pastry cutter. Cook, in batches, in a large saucepan of rapidly boiling salted water for 6 minutes each batch. Drain well and return to the pan to keep warm.

To make the sauce, melt the butter in a saucepan, add the flour, and cook over low heat for 2 minutes. Remove from the heat and gradually stir in the combined milk, cream, and wine. Cook over low heat until the sauce begins to

thicken, stirring constantly to prevent lumps from forming. Bring to the boil and simmer gently for 5 minutes. Add the parmesan and parsley and stir until combined. Remove from the heat, add to the ravioli, and toss well.

Sauce

heaping ¼ cup butter

3 tablespoons all-purpose flour

1½ cups milk

1¼ cups whipping cream

½ cup dry white wine

½ cup freshly grated parmesan cheese

2 tablespoons chopped flat-leaf parsley

NOTE The pasta dough should be set aside for 30 minutes to let the gluten in the flour relax. If you don't do this, you run the risk of making tough pasta.

Pasta, Rice, & Noodles

79

Serves
8

Classic lasagna

2 tablespoons oil

2 tablespoons butter

1 large onion, finely chopped

1 carrot, finely chopped

1 celery stalk, finely chopped

1 pound ground beef

5½ ounces chicken livers,
  finely chopped

1 cup puréed tomatoes

1 cup red wine

2 tablespoons chopped
  flat-leaf parsley

13 ounces fresh lasagna sheets

1 cup freshly grated parmesan
  cheese

Béchamel sauce

¼ cup butter

⅓ cup all-purpose flour

2¼ cups milk

½ teaspoon freshly grated
  nutmeg

This layered dish of meat, pasta, and creamy béchamel sauce is possibly the classic diet-breaker. If you prefer, you can leave out the chicken livers and increase the amount of ground beef.

Heat the oil and butter in a heavy-based frying pan and cook the onion, carrot, and celery over medium heat until softened, stirring constantly. Increase the heat, add the beef, and brown well, breaking up any lumps with a fork. Add the chicken livers and cook until they change color. Add the tomato passata, wine, and parsley, and season to taste. Bring to the boil, reduce the heat and simmer for 45 minutes, then set aside.

To make the béchamel sauce, melt the butter in a saucepan over low heat. Add the flour and stir for 1 minute. Remove from the heat and gradually stir in the milk. Return to the heat and stir constantly until the sauce boils and begins to thicken. Simmer for another minute. Add the nutmeg and season to taste. Place a piece of plastic wrap on the surface of the sauce to prevent a skin from forming, and set aside.

Cut the lasagne sheets to fit into a deep, rectangular ovenproof dish.

To assemble, preheat the oven to 350°F. Grease the ovenproof dish. Spread a thin layer of the meat sauce over the base and follow with a thin layer of béchamel. If the béchamel has cooled and become too thick, warm it gently to make spreading easier. Lay the lasagne sheets on top, gently pressing to push out any air. Continue the layers, finishing with the béchamel. Sprinkle with parmesan and bake for 35–40 minutes, or until golden brown. Cool for 15 minutes before cutting.

Pad thai

Serves 4–6

9 ounces dried rice stick noodles

1 tablespoon tamarind purée

1 small red chili, chopped

2 garlic cloves, chopped

2 scallions, sliced

1½ tablespoons sugar

2 tablespoons fish sauce

2 tablespoons lime juice

2 tablespoons oil

2 eggs, beaten

8 large uncooked shrimp

6 ounces pork fillet, thinly sliced

4 ounces fried tofu puffs, cut into thin strips

1 cup bean sprouts

¼ cup chopped roasted peanuts

3 tablespoons cilantro leaves

1 lime, cut into wedges

Put the noodles in a heatproof bowl, cover with warm water, and soak for 15–20 minutes, or until soft and pliable. Drain well.

Combine the tamarind purée with 1 tablespoon water. Put the chili, garlic, and scallions in a spice grinder or mortar and pestle, and grind to a smooth paste. Transfer the mixture to a bowl. Stir in the tamarind mixture along with the sugar, fish sauce, and lime juice, stirring until combined.

Heat a wok until very hot, add 1 tablespoon of the oil, and swirl to coat the base and side. Add the egg, swirl to coat, and cook for 1–2 minutes, or until set. Remove, roll up, and cut into thin slices.

Peel the shrimp and gently pull out the dark vein from each shrimp back, starting from the head end.

Heat the remaining oil in the wok, stir in the chili mixture, and stir-fry for 30 seconds. Add the pork and stir-fry for 2 minutes, or until tender. Add the shrimp and stir-fry for a further minute, or until pink and curled.

Stir in the noodles, egg, tofu, and bean sprouts. and gently toss everything together until heated through. Serve at once topped with the peanuts, cilantro, and lime wedges.

Serves
4

Seafood risotto

2 ripe tomatoes

1 pound black mussels

1¼ cups dry white wine

5 cups fish stock

pinch saffron threads

2 tablespoons olive oil

2 tablespoons butter

1 pound uncooked shrimp,
    peeled and deveined

8 ounces squid tubes, sliced
    into thin rings

7 ounces scallops

3 garlic cloves, crushed

1 onion, finely chopped

2 cups risotto rice

2 tablespoons chopped
    flat-leaf parsley

Score a cross in the base of each tomato. Put in a heatproof bowl and cover with boiling water. Leave for 30 seconds, then transfer to cold water and peel the skin away from the cross. Chop the tomato flesh.

Scrub the mussels with a stiff brush and pull out the hairy beards. Discard any broken mussels, or open ones that don't close when tapped. Rinse well. Pour the wine into a large saucepan and bring to the boil. Add the mussels and cook, covered, over medium heat for 3–5 minutes, or until the mussels open. Discard any unopened mussels. Strain, reserving the liquid. Remove the mussels from their shells. Combine the mussel liquid, stock, and saffron in a saucepan, cover, and keep at a low simmer.

Heat the oil and butter in a saucepan over medium heat. Add the prawns and cook until pink. Remove. Add the squid and scallops and cook for about 1–2 minutes, until white. Remove. Add the garlic and onion and cook for 3 minutes, or until golden. Add the rice and stir. Add ½ cup of the hot liquid, stirring until it is all absorbed. Continue adding liquid, ½ cup at a time, stirring, for 25 minutes, or until the liquid is absorbed. Stir in the tomato, seafood, and parsley and heat through. Season to taste with salt and black pepper.

82

Serves
4–6

Spaghetti bolognese

2 tablespoons olive oil

2 garlic cloves, crushed

1 large onion, chopped

1 carrot, chopped

1 celery stalk, chopped

1 pound ground beef

2 cups beef stock

1½ cups red wine

3⅓ cups canned crushed
    tomatoes

1 teaspoon sugar

3 tablespoons chopped
    flat-leaf parsley

1 pound spaghetti

freshly grated parmesan
    cheese, to serve

Heat the olive oil in a large deep frying pan. Add the garlic, onion, carrot, and celery, and stir for 5 minutes over low heat until the vegetables are golden.

Increase the heat, add the beef, and brown well, stirring and breaking up any lumps with a fork as it cooks. Add the stock, wine, tomato, sugar, and parsley.

Bring the mixture to the boil, reduce the heat, and simmer for 1½ hours, stirring occasionally. Season to taste.

Shortly before serving, cook the pasta in a large saucepan of rapidly boiling salted water until al dente. Drain and then divide among serving bowls. Serve the sauce over the top of the pasta and sprinkle with the parmesan.

NOTE Long, slow cooking is essential to give maximum flavor to this dish. If you have time, cook it for longer than specified, either on the stovetop or in a casserole dish in a low oven. Stir it occasionally and add a little more stock or wine if the liquid reduces too much.

83

12 mussels

Tomato sauce

2 tablespoons olive oil

1 onion, finely diced

1 carrot, sliced

1 red chili, seeded and chopped

2 garlic cloves, crushed

1¾ cups canned crushed tomatoes

½ cup dry white wine

1 teaspoon sugar

pinch cayenne pepper

¼ cup white wine

¼ cup fish stock

1 garlic clove, crushed

13 ounces spaghetti

2 tablespoons butter

5 ounces small squid tubes, sliced

5 ounces boneless white fish fillets, cubed

7 ounces raw prawns (shrimp), peeled and deveined

1 large handful flat-leaf parsley, chopped

7 ounces canned clams, drained

Spaghetti marinara

Scrub the mussels with a stiff brush and pull out the hairy beards. Discard any broken mussels, or any open ones that don't close when tapped on a work surface. Rinse well.

To make the tomato sauce, heat the oil in a saucepan, add the onion and carrot, and stir over medium heat for about 10 minutes, or until the vegetables are lightly browned. Add the chili, garlic, tomato, white wine, sugar, and cayenne pepper. Simmer for 30 minutes, stirring occasionally.

Meanwhile, heat the wine with the stock and garlic in a large saucepan and add the unopened mussels. Cover the pan and shake it over high heat for 3–5 minutes. After 3 minutes, start removing any opened mussels and set them aside. After 5 minutes, discard any unopened mussels and reserve the wine mixture.

Cook the pasta in a large saucepan of rapidly boiling salted water until al dente. Drain and keep warm. Meanwhile, melt the butter in a frying pan, add the squid rings, fish, and prawns and stir-fry for 2 minutes. Set aside. Add the reserved wine mixture, mussels, squid, fish, prawns, parsley, and clams to the tomato sauce and reheat gently. Gently combine the sauce with the pasta and serve at once.

84

Singapore noodles

Serves
4–6

6 ounces dried rice vermicelli

oil, for cooking

9 ounces Chinese barbecued pork (char siu), cut into small pieces

9 ounces uncooked shrimp, peeled and cut into small pieces

2 tablespoons hot curry powder

2 garlic cloves, crushed

1 onion, thinly sliced

10 shiitake mushrooms, thinly sliced

¾ cup green beans, thinly sliced on the diagonal

1 tablespoon soy sauce

4 scallions, thinly sliced on the diagonal

Place the vermicelli in a large bowl, cover with boiling water, and soak for 5 minutes. Drain well and spread out on a clean dish towel to dry.

Heat a wok or large frying pan until very hot, add 1 tablespoon oil, and swirl it around to coat the side. Stir-fry the pork and the shrimp pieces in batches over high heat. Remove from the wok.

Reheat the wok, add 2 tablespoons of the oil, and stir-fry the curry powder and garlic for 1–2 minutes, or until fragrant. Add the onion and mushrooms and stir-fry over medium heat for 2–3 minutes, or until the onion and mushrooms are soft.

Return the pork and shrimp to the wok, add the beans and 2 teaspoons water, and toss to combine. Add the drained noodles, soy sauce, and scallions. Toss well and serve.

⅓ cup olive oil

9 ounces pork spare ribs, cut into ½-inch thick slices

I brown onion, chopped

½ cup puréed tomatoes

I teaspoon sweet paprika (pimentón)

3½ ounces fresh spicy pork sausages, thickly sliced

3½ ounces chorizo, sliced

6 cups beef or chicken stock

I pound spaghettini, broken into I-inch pieces

Picada

⅓ cup nuts (hazelnuts, pine nuts, or almonds)

2 garlic cloves, crushed

2 tablespoons chopped flat-leaf parsley

¼ teaspoon ground cinnamon

I slice bread, toasted and crusts removed

¼ teaspoon saffron threads

Spanish noodles

Heat the oil in a large heavy-based saucepan over medium–high heat and cook the ribs in batches until golden. Add the onion and cook for 5 minutes, or until softened. Stir in the tomato and paprika and cook for a few minutes more.

Add the pork sausages, chorizo, and all but 2 tablespoons of the stock and bring to the boil. Reduce to a simmer and add the spaghettini. Cook, covered, for 15 minutes, or until the pasta is al dente.

Meanwhile, to make the picada, in a mortar and pestle or food processor, crush the nuts with the garlic, parsley, cinnamon, and bread to make a paste. Stir in the saffron. If the mixture is too dry, add 1–2 tablespoons of the reserved stock. Stir into the casserole and simmer for 5 minutes, or until the casserole has thickened slightly. Season well before serving.

Seafood paella

½ cup white wine

I red onion, chopped

12 black mussels, debearded and scrubbed (see page 174)

½ cup olive oil

½ red onion, extra, finely chopped

I thick slice of jamón, finely chopped

4 garlic cloves, crushed

I red bell pepper, finely chopped

I ripe tomato, peeled, seeded, and chopped

3¼ ounces chorizo, thinly sliced

pinch of cayenne pepper

I cup paella or medium-grain rice

¼ teaspoon saffron threads

2 cups chicken stock, heated

½ cup fresh or frozen peas

12 uncooked shrimp, peeled and deveined

2 squid tubes, cleaned and cut into rings

4 ounces skinless firm white fish fillets, cut into pieces

2 tablespoons finely chopped flat-leaf parsley

Heat the wine and onion in a saucepan over high heat. Add the mussels, cover, and gently shake the pan for 5–8 minutes. Remove from the heat, discard any closed mussels, and drain, reserving the liquid.

Heat the oil in a large heavy-based frying pan, add the extra onion, jamón, garlic, and bell pepper, and cook for about 5 minutes. Add the chopped tomato, chorizo, and cayenne pepper. Season. Stir in the reserved liquid, then add the rice and stir again.

Blend the saffron with the hot stock, then stir into the rice mixture. Bring to the boil, then reduce the heat to low and simmer, uncovered, for 15 minutes without stirring.

Put the peas, shrimp, squid, and fish on top of the rice. Push them in, cover, and cook over low heat for 10 minutes, turning them over halfway through, until the rice is tender and the seafood is cooked through. Add the mussels for the last 5 minutes to heat through. If the rice is not quite cooked, add a little extra stock and cook for a few more minutes. Leave to rest for 5 minutes, then add the parsley and serve.

Vegetarian PLATES

Serves
6

Pumpkin soup with harissa

5 pounds winter squash

3 cups vegetable stock

3 cups milk

sugar, to taste

Harissa

9 ounces fresh or dried red chilies

1 tablespoon caraway seeds

1 tablespoon coriander seeds

2 teaspoons cumin seeds

4–6 garlic cloves

1 tablespoon dried mint

½ cup extra virgin olive oil

Remove the skin, seeds, and fiber from the squash and cut into pieces. Simmer, uncovered, in a large saucepan with the stock and milk for 15–20 minutes or until tender. Allow to cool slightly before transferring to a food processor and blending, in batches, until smooth. Season with a little sugar and black pepper. Return to a clean saucepan and gently reheat until ready to serve.

To make the harissa, wearing rubber gloves, remove the stems of the chilies, split the chilies in half, remove the seeds, and soften the flesh in hot water for 5 minutes (or 30 minutes if using dried chilies). Drain and place in a food processor.

While the chilies are soaking, dry-fry the caraway, coriander, and cumin seeds in an ungreased frying pan for 1–2 minutes, or until they become aromatic. Add the seeds, garlic, mint, and 1 teaspoon salt to the food processor and, slowly adding the olive oil, process until a smooth, thick paste forms. Stir a little harissa into individual bowls of soup to suit each diner's taste.

NOTES Harissa is a chili paste widely used as a condiment throughout North Africa.

It's good practice to wear disposable rubber gloves while preparing this dish, or any dish containing chilies. This will prevent your hands from picking up the irritants in the chilies and then possibly transferring them to your eyes or skin.

Serves
4

Baked cheese and spinach cannelloni

Tomato sauce

2 tablespoons olive oil

1 large onion, finely chopped

2 garlic cloves, finely
chopped

2 pounds canned tomatoes,
roughly chopped

2 rosemary sprigs

2 bay leaves

2 tablespoons concentrated
tomato purée

1 pound English spinach

heaped 1 cup feta cheese,
crumbled

2/3 cup ricotta cheese

½ cup freshly grated
parmesan cheese

2 tablespoons finely chopped
mint

2 eggs, lightly beaten

2 tablespoons pine nuts,
toasted

16 instant cannelloni tubes

1⅓ cups finely grated
mozzarella cheese

To make the tomato sauce, heat the olive oil in a large pan.
Add the onion and garlic, and cook over medium heat until
the onion is soft. Stir in the tomato, herbs, and tomato
purée. Bring to the boil, reduce the heat, and simmer for
25–30 minutes, or until the sauce is thick. Season to taste.
Remove the bay leaves and rosemary sprigs and discard.

Preheat the oven to 400°F. Wash the spinach and remove
the stems. Steam until just wilted. Drain thoroughly,
squeeze out as much water as possible, and chop roughly.
Combine the spinach with the cheeses, mint, eggs, and pine
nuts, and season with salt and freshly ground black pepper.
Mix thoroughly. Using a small spoon or a knife, carefully
fill the cannelloni tubes.

Spoon some tomato sauce over the base of a large, shallow
baking dish. Arrange the cannelloni tubes on top. Cover
with the remaining tomato sauce and mozzarella. Bake for
30–40 minutes, or until the top is golden and the pasta
is tender.

NOTES When buying ricotta cheese, choose bulk
ricotta from the deli counter; it has a firmer texture
and more distinctive flavor than the smooth ricotta
sold in tubs.

To toast pine nuts, put them in a small, dry frying
pan or saucepan and stir over low–medium heat until
they are fragrant and lightly golden. Transfer to a
small dish so they do not cook further in the residual
heat of the pan.

Serves
4

Gado gado

6 new potatoes

2 carrots, cut into batons

9 ounces yard-long beans,
cut into long lengths

2 tablespoons peanut oil

1 1/3 cups firm tofu, cubed

2 short cucumbers, cut into
batons

1 large red bell pepper, cut
into batons

3/4 cup bean sprouts

5 hard-cooked eggs

Peanut sauce

1 tablespoon peanut oil

1 onion, finely chopped

2/3 cup peanut butter

1/4 cup kecap manis

2 tablespoons ground
coriander

2 teaspoons chili sauce

3/4 cup coconut cream

1 teaspoon grated palm sugar
(jaggery)

1 tablespoon lemon juice

A platter of crisp, fresh vegetables seems such a healthful prospect—until you serve it with a big bowl of dipping sauce made from coconut cream and peanut butter. Oh well, at least you'll still be getting plenty of vitamins.

Boil the potatoes until tender. Drain and cool slightly. Cut into quarters. Cook the carrot and beans separately in boiling water until just tender. Plunge into iced water to stop further cooking, then drain.

Heat the oil in a nonstick frying pan and cook the tofu in batches. Drain on paper towels.

To make the peanut sauce, heat the oil in a frying pan over low heat and cook the onion for about 5 minutes. Add the peanut butter, kecap manis, coriander, chili sauce, and coconut cream. Bring to the boil, reduce the heat, and simmer for 5 minutes. Stir in the palm sugar and lemon juice until the sugar has dissolved. Arrange the vegetables and tofu on a plate. Halve the eggs and place in the center. Serve with the sauce.

NOTES Kecap manis is a thick, sweet Indonesian soy sauce. It can be found in Asian grocery stores and large supermarkets.

If palm sugar (jaggery) is unavailable, it can be replaced with dark brown sugar.

Risotto primavera

6 cups vegetable stock

2 tablespoons olive oil

¼ cup butter

1 large onion, finely chopped

1 carrot, finely diced

2 garlic cloves, crushed

2 cups risotto rice

7 ounces thin asparagus, cut into ¾-inch pieces

2 small zucchini, thinly sliced

¾ cup fresh peas

½ cup chopped flat-leaf parsley

½ cup freshly grated parmesan cheese

Pour the stock into a saucepan and bring to the boil. Reduce the heat, cover with a lid, and keep at a low simmer.

Heat the oil and half the butter in a large, heavy-based saucepan over medium heat. Add the onion and carrot, and stir for 5 minutes. Add the garlic and cook, stirring, for 2 minutes, or until the onion is softened. Stir in the rice until well coated.

Add ½ cup of the hot stock. Stir constantly over medium heat until nearly all the liquid is absorbed. Continue adding the stock, ½ cup at a time, stirring. After 10 minutes, add the asparagus, zucchini, and peas. Continue adding the remaining stock. Cook for a further 10—15 minutes, or until the rice is tender and creamy.

Remove from the heat and stir in the parsley, parmesan, and remaining butter. Season to taste.

91

Serves
4

Cheese and spinach pancakes

9 ounces cooked English spinach, squeezed dry and chopped (about 1 pound 5 ounces uncooked weight; or use 9 ounces frozen spinach, thawed and the water squeezed out)

½ cup fresh curd cheese

¼ cup grated cheddar cheese

a pinch of nutmeg

¼ cup grated parmesan cheese

½ teaspoon paprika

½ cup fresh breadcrumbs

batter

1 cup all-purpose flour

1¼ cups milk

1 egg, lightly beaten

butter, for cooking

cheese sauce

2 tablespoons butter

¼ cup all-purpose flour

1¾ cups milk

1 cup grated cheddar cheese

Grease a large ovenproof dish.

Combine the spinach, curd cheese, cheddar, nutmeg, and freshly ground pepper, to taste, in a bowl and mix well.

To make the pancake batter, sift the flour and a pinch of salt into a bowl. Add half the milk and the egg. Whisk until smooth, then whisk in the remaining milk.

Heat a teaspoon of butter in a frying pan over medium heat and slowly pour in the batter to create a thin layer in the base of the pan. Cook for 2–3 minutes, or until golden, then turn over and cook the other side. Repeat to make 8 pancakes.

To make the cheese sauce, melt the butter over low heat, add the flour, and cook for 1 minute. Stirring constantly over medium heat, gradually add the milk, bringing the mixture back to a simmer between additions and stirring well to prevent lumps from forming. Cook until the mixture thickens, then remove from the heat, season to taste with salt and pepper, and stir in the grated cheese.

Preheat the oven to 350°F. Divide the spinach filling among the pancakes, roll the pancakes up, then place in the prepared dish. Pour the cheese sauce over the pancakes. Combine the parmesan, paprika, and breadcrumbs in a bowl then sprinkle over the sauce. Bake for 30 minutes, or until golden brown. Serve immediately.

Serves 4–6

Linguine pesto

2 cups firmly packed basil
  leaves

2 garlic cloves, crushed

¼ cup pine nuts, toasted

¾ cup olive oil

½ cup freshly grated
  parmesan cheese, plus
  extra, to serve

1 pound 2 ounces linguine

It's the pine nuts, cheese, and liberal amount of olive oil that tip this recipe right over the edge—not to mention all the carbs from the linguine. But it's one of the simplest and most delicious of all pastas, so every excess calorie seems well worth it.

Process the basil, garlic, and pine nuts together in a food processor. With the motor running, add the oil in a steady stream until mixed to a smooth paste. Transfer to a bowl, stir in the parmesan, and season to taste.

Cook the pasta in a large saucepan of rapidly boiling salted water until al dente. Drain and return to the pan. Toss enough of the pesto through the pasta to coat it well. Serve sprinkled with parmesan.

NOTE Refrigerate any leftover pesto in an airtight jar for up to a week. Cover the surface with a layer of oil. Freeze for up to 1 month.

Serves 4

Chili noodles and nuts

1½ tablespoons oil

1 tablespoon sesame oil

2–3 small red chilies, finely chopped

1 large onion, cut into thin wedges

4 garlic cloves, very thinly sliced

1 red and 1 green bell pepper, cut into strips, plus extra finely sliced, to garnish

2 large carrots, cut into batons

3½ ounces green beans

2 celery stalks, cut into batons

2 teaspoons honey

1 pound 2 ounces egg noodles, gently separated

⅔ cup dry-roasted peanuts

⅔ cup honey-roasted cashews

4 scallions, chopped

sweet chili sauce and sesame oil, to serve

Heat the wok over low heat, add the oils, and swirl them to coat the side. When the oil is warm, add the chili and heat until the oil is very hot.

Add the onion and garlic and stir-fry for 1 minute, or until the onion just softens. Add the bell pepper, carrot, and beans and stir-fry for 1 minute. Add the celery, honey, and 1 tablespoon water, and season with salt and pepper. Toss well, then cover and cook for 1–2 minutes, or until the vegetables are just tender.

Add the noodles and nuts and toss well. Cook, covered, for 1–2 minutes, or until the noodles are heated through. Stir in the scallions and serve, drizzled with the sweet chili sauce and sesame oil. Garnish with the finely sliced bell pepper.

94

Serves
4

Red vegetable curry

1 tablespoon oil

1 medium onion, chopped

1–2 tablespoons red curry
  paste (opposite; or use a
  bought curry paste)

1½ cups coconut milk

2 medium potatoes (about
  10 ounces), chopped

1¼ cups cauliflower florets

6 makrut (kaffir lime) leaves

1¼ cups yard-long beans, cut
  into 1¼ inch pieces

½ red bell pepper, cut into
  strips

10 fresh baby corn spears,
  cut in half lengthways

1 tablespoons green
  peppercorns, roughly
  chopped

¼ cup fresh Thai basil leaves,
  finely chopped

2 tablespoons soy sauce

1 tablespoon lime juice

2 teaspoons soft brown sugar

Heat the oil in a large wok or frying pan. Cook the onion
and curry paste for 4 minutes over medium heat, stirring.

Add the coconut milk and 1 cup water, bring to the boil
and simmer, uncovered, for 5 minutes. Add the potato,
cauliflower, and makrut leaves, and simmer for 7 minutes.
Add the beans, bell pepper, corn, and peppercorns, and
cook for 5 minutes, or until the vegetables are tender.

Stir through the basil, soy sauce, lime juice, and sugar.
Serve with steamed rice.

NOTE If you don't want to make your
own curry paste, there are good commercial
versions avaialable. Some contain shrimp
paste; if you are a strict vegetarian, check the
ingredients list before buying. Some vegetarian
versions use soy sauce instead.

To make the red curry paste, place the coriander and cumin seeds in a dry frying pan and roast over medium heat for 2–3 minutes, shaking the pan constantly.

Place the roasted spices and peppercorns in a mortar and pound with a pestle until finely ground, or process in a spice grinder.

Wrap the shrimp paste, if using, in a small piece of foil and cook under a hot broiler for 3 minutes, turning the package twice.

Place the ground spices, shrimp paste, nutmeg, and chili in a food processor and process for 5 seconds. Add the remaining ingredients and process for 20 seconds at a time, scraping down the sides of the bowl each time, until a smooth paste is formed. Use as instructed in the recipe.

Leftover curry paste can be stored in an airtight container in the refrigerator for up to 1 week, or frozen for up to 1 month.

Red curry paste

1 tablespoon coriander seeds

2 teaspoons cumin seeds

1 teaspoon black peppercorns

2 teaspoons shrimp paste (optional)

1 teaspoon ground nutmeg

12 dried or fresh red chilies, roughly chopped

20 red Asian shallots, chopped

2 tablespoons oil

4 stems lemon grass (white part only), finely chopped

12 small cloves garlic, chopped

2 tablespoons chopped fresh cilantro roots

2 cilantro chopped fresh coriander stem

6 makrut (kaffir lime) leaves, chopped

2 teaspoons grated lime rind

2 teaspoons salt

2 teaspoons ground turmeric

1 teaspoon paprika

95

Serves
4

Pasta boscaiola

1 pound pasta (see Note)

1 tablespoon olive oil

2¼ cups sliced button mushrooms

2½ cups whipping cream

2 scallions, sliced

1 tablespoon chopped parsley

Cook the pasta in a large saucepan of rapidly boiling salted water until al dente. Drain well and return to the pan to keep warm.

Meanwhile, heat the oil in a large frying pan, add the mushrooms, and cook, stirring, for 5 minutes, or until golden brown.

Add a little of the cream and stir well with a wooden spoon. Add the remaining cream, bring to the boil, and cook over high heat for 15 minutes, or until thick enough to coat the back of a spoon. Add the scallions. Pour the sauce over the pasta and toss well. Serve sprinkled with the parsley.

NOTE Boscaiola sauce usually contains bacon, so you can add some vegetarian bacon to this recipe if you like it.

This sauce is normally served with spaghetti, but you can use any pasta. We have shown it with casarecce. If you are short on time and don't have 15 minutes to reduce the sauce, it can be thickened with 2 teaspoons of cornstarch mixed with 1 tablespoon of water. Stir until the mixture boils and thickens.

Pizza margherita

1½ cups white bread flour

1 teaspoon sugar

2 teaspoons dried yeast

1 tablespoon olive oil, plus
    extra to oil the bowl

⅓ cup plus 1 tablespoon milk

Topping

1 tablespoon olive oil

1 garlic clove, crushed

15 ounces canned crushed
    tomatoes

1 bay leaf

1 teaspoon chopped thyme

6 chopped basil leaves

cornmeal, to sprinkle

1 cup thinly sliced fresh baby
    mozzarella cheese

olive oil, extra, to drizzle

To make the pizza crust, put the flour, sugar, yeast, and
½ teaspoon salt in a large bowl. Stir together the olive oil,
milk, and ⅓ cup warm water and add to the bowl. Stir with
a wooden spoon.

Place on a lightly floured work surface and knead for
5 minutes, or until soft and smooth. Lightly oil a large
bowl, add the dough, and turn to coat in the oil. Leave
in a warm place for 1 hour, or until doubled in size.
Preheat the oven to 415°F.

To make the topping, heat the oil in a saucepan over
medium heat, add the garlic, and stir for 30 seconds.
Add the tomatoes, bay leaf, thyme, and basil, and simmer,
stirring occasionally, for 20–25 minutes, or until thick.
Cool, then remove the bay leaf.

Place the dough on a floured work surface, punch down
to expel the air, and knead for 5 minutes. Shape into a
neat ball and roll to 11–12 inches in diameter. Oil a pizza
tray the size of the dough. Sprinkle the tray with polenta
and place the dough on top. Spread the sauce over the
dough, leaving a 1¼-inch border. Arrange the sliced cheese
over the top and drizzle with olive oil. Bake for 15 minutes,
or until crisp and bubbling.

97

Serves
4

Macaroni and cheese

1⅓ cups macaroni

¼ cup butter

1 onion, chopped

¼ cup all-purpose flour

2½ cups milk

½ teaspoon nutmeg

1½ cups grated cheddar cheese

Dried breadcrumbs, for sprinkling

Preheat the oven to 350°F. Grease a 5-cup ovenproof dish. Cook the macaroni in rapidly boiling water until tender, then drain.

Heat the butter in a large pan, add the onion, and stir over medium heat for 4 minutes, or until soft. Add the flour and stir over low heat for 1 minute. Remove from the heat and gradually add the milk. Stir until smooth. Return to medium heat and cook over low heat for 1 minute. Remove from the heat and stir in the nutmeg. Season with salt and freshly ground black pepper.

Stir the pasta and two-thirds of the cheese to the sauce. Spoon the mixture into the dish, sprinkle with the remaining cheese and a generous handful of breadcrumbs, and bake for 20 minutes, or until golden.

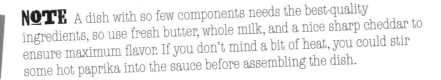

NOTE A dish with so few components needs the best-quality ingredients, so use fresh butter, whole milk, and a nice sharp cheddar to ensure maximum flavor. If you don't mind a bit of heat, you could stir some hot paprika into the sauce before assembling the dish.

Twice-baked cheese soufflés

1 cup milk

3 whole black peppercorns

1 onion, cut in half and
   studded with 2 cloves

1 bay leaf

¼ cup butter

½ cup self-raising flour

2 eggs, separated

1 cup grated gruyère cheese

1 cup whipping cream

½ cup finely grated parmesan
   cheese

Preheat the oven to 350°F. Lightly grease four ½-cup
ramekins.

Place the milk, peppercorns, onion, and bay leaf in a
saucepan and heat until nearly boiling. Remove from
the heat and let the milk infuse for 10 minutes. Strain,
discarding the solids.

Melt the butter in a saucepan, add the flour, and cook over
medium heat for 1 minute. Stirring constantly, add the milk
a little at a time, returning the mixture to a simmer between
additions and stirring well to prevent lumps from forming.
Simmer, stirring, until the mixture boils and thickens.

Transfer the mixture to a bowl, add the egg yolks and
gruyère cheese, and stir to combine well.

Using electric beaters, whisk the egg whites until soft peaks
form, then gently fold into the cheese sauce. Divide the
mixture among the ramekins and place in a baking dish
half-filled with hot water. Bake for 15 minutes. Remove
from the baking dish, cool, and refrigerate until needed.

Preheat the oven to 400°F, remove the soufflés from
the ramekins, and place onto ovenproof plates. Pour the
cream over the top and sprinkle with parmesan. Bake for
20 minutes, or until puffed and golden. Serve immediately.

Serves
4

Gnocchi romana

3 cups milk

½ teaspoon freshly grated
   nutmeg

⅔ cup semolina

1 egg, beaten

1½ cups freshly grated
   parmesan cheese

¼ cup melted butter

½ cup whipping cream

½ cup freshly grated
   mozzarella cheese

Any dish containing cheese is likely to tip the balance from sensible to foolish fairly quickly. This dish, with two types of cheese plus butter, cream, and plenty of milk, is no exception. But who's going to say no when the result is so delicious?

Line a deep jelly roll pan with baking paper. Combine the milk and half the nutmeg in a saucepan and season to taste. Bring to the boil, reduce the heat, and gradually stir in the semolina. Cook, stirring occasionally, for 5–10 minutes, or until the semolina is very stiff.

Remove the pan from the heat, add the egg and 1 cup of the parmesan cheese. Stir to combine and then spread the mixture in the prepared pan. Refrigerate for 1 hour, or until the mixture is firm.

Preheat the oven to 350°F. Lightly grease a shallow casserole dish. Cut the semolina into rounds using a floured 1½-inch cutter and arrange in the dish.

Pour the melted butter over the top, then the cream. Combine the remaining parmesan with the mozzarella and sprinkle the mixture on the rounds. Sprinkle with the remaining nutmeg. Bake for 20–25 minutes, or until the mixture is golden.

100

Serves
4

Fried tofu, choy sum and baby corn

2 tablespoons peanut oil

14 ounces deep-fried
tofu puffs, halved

4 tablespoons mushroom
sauce or vegetarian oyster
sauce (see Note)

2 tablespoons light soy sauce

2 tablespoons sweet chili
sauce

2 tablespoons honey

2 garlic cloves, crushed

12 baby corn, halved
lengthways

1 pound choy sum leaves, cut
into short lengths

Heat a wok over high heat, add the oil, and swirl to coat the side. Add the tofu puffs and stir-fry for 2 minutes, or until crisp and golden.

Place all the sauces and the honey in a small bowl and mix together well.

Add the garlic, baby corn, and choy sum to the wok and pour in the combined sauce, along with ¼ cup water. Stir-fry for 3–4 minutes, or until the leaves have just wilted. Serve immediately.

NOTE Vegetarian "oyster" sauce is made from mushrooms, not oysters. It may be labelled mushroom sauce or vegetarian mushroom sauce.